Yesterday Today

In the Ozarks

Yesterday Today

Life in the Ozarks

By

CATHERINE S. BARKER

Illustrated With Photographs

The

1941

Printed, lithographed, and bound in the United States of America by
The CAXTON PRINTERS, Ltd.
Caldwell, Idaho
55713

TO MY PARENTS

GEORGE BEATY and ANNA FURRY SWEAZEY

whose faith has been a constant source of inspiration

Preface

IN ISOLATED SECTIONS OF THE OZARK MOUNTAINS there are still remnants of eighteenth-century life and culture. Little note has been taken of this fact. It seems high time to fix the present situation in some permanent form, for, as roads are extended and improved and radios are more widely used, true isolation areas are shrinking.

The people of whom this is written will not read this book. Readers who live in the Ozarks may say, "I never saw anything like that." I would remind them that when many persons know of these isolated places they will no longer be isolated. It is probable that they will also say, "The writer is describing conditions as they were fifty years ago." For their towns that may be true. If they lived in some other locality they might truly say "one hundred years ago," or even "two hundred." The degree to which these facts are true of any community or family today depends upon the duration and extent of their contact with the outside world.

I am writing not of things I have read nor of things I have heard, but of things I have seen, of people with whom I have talked recently, of conditions I know to be true at present.

For a number of years I had lived in a college

town in the foothills of the Ozarks, seeing and
wondering about the mountaineers, but with no
chance of knowing them. Then, as a case worker
for the Federal Emergency Relief Administration, I was sent into the mountains to visit many
homes. Applicants for relief anxiously awaited
my coming. They were eager to show me their
houses and to tell me in great detail of their circumstances. I was not regarded with suspicion
as a prying outsider. Because they knew why I
came, I was welcomed and trusted. I visited not
only relief applicants, but I called on their more
fortunate neighbors, to ask about the roads or to
get supplementary information about clients.
These people, too, knew my business and were
gracious and hospitable. Consequently I was afforded a remarkable opportunity to learn much
of living conditions, customs, and speech, which
it is ordinarily practically impossible for a stranger to discover. And I found the people to be
well worth knowing and their way of life to be
fascinating.

No attempt is made to depict a typical mountaineer. That would seem as foolish as to try to
describe a typical urbanite. To any person his
friends and the way of life he knows are typical.
Modes of living are recounted as I have found them
among the poverty-stricken and the "better fixed."
In the Ozarks the economic distance between the
two is slight. Extreme or unique instances are
labeled as such. In addition to looking around the
farm, the reader is taken into a number of homes,
into the main room, the kitchen, and the sickroom.

He is given time to sit by the fire with the family in order that he may become acquainted with the mountaineer as he is—lovable and pathetic and needy and self-satisfied and valiant.

It is hoped that many sorts of persons may profit by meeting him. He offers a wonderful laboratory demonstration for students of early American history—living life today as it was lived in yesteryears. He offers an example, for the student of sociology, of the effect of almost complete isolation, with intermarriage, and with his standards and mores ingrown. For the economist he has a modified barter system and outmoded methods of production. To those interested in the moral and spiritual development of a retarded people he presents an urgent problem. And for all who enjoy people and a view of other ways of life, he is an interesting person to meet.

In assembling this material far from the Ozarks, I owe much to Mary McIntosh Burnett, companion of some of my mountain jaunts, who has supplied many facts, gathered pictures, and read the manuscript.

Sincere thanks are due, also to Lula G. Parse, a true friend of the mountaineers, who helped me to know them and their needs; to J. G. Edmonds for his sound advice and his encouragement; to Vance Randolph, author and authority on Ozark life, who has read the entire manuscript and given many valuable suggestions; to Agnes Walker, Nurse-in-charge at the Presbyterian Health Center of Mt. Pleasant, Arkansas, for a variety of material and pictures; to many others in widely scattered parts of the Ozarks, for information and answers to questions; and to a number who have read parts of the manuscript which they were particularly qualified to criticize.

Pictures have been generously supplied, also, by Opal B. Rodgers, the Farm Security Administration, the Batesville Chamber of Commerce, and the Office of Education and Publicity of the Board of National Missions of the Presbyterian Church, U. S. A. The pictures illustrate various types. Those taken by the FSA represent destitute families. Some of the others are of persons and homes near the top of the economic scale.

Grateful acknowledgment is made for permission granted by a number of authors and publishers to adapt bits of relevant information found in their works.

For the Indian legends, some facts of early history, derivations of place names, and superstitions, I am indebted to Fred W. Allsopp, author of *Folklore of Romantic Arkansas*, published by the Grolier Society, of Kansas City, Missouri.

Other superstitions were found in the *Arkansas Gazette* (Little Rock) and the Batesville *Guard*, especially in articles by Mary Elizabeth Overholt, in the *Gazette*, and by Paul T. Wayland, in the *Guard*.

Interesting Ozark stories and expressions are included in the little book, *Over the Old Ozark Trails*, by Pearl Spurlock, and in Karr Shannon's *Hillbilly Philosophy*.

The bits of verse at the chapter heads are from *Children's Mother Goose* and are used by permis-

sion of the Reilly and Lee Company, of Chicago.
Some of these verses are thought to have originated
at about the same period as the old culture which
survives in the Ozarks today.

Contents

Illustrations

Prologue

OFTTIMES IN DAYS OF OLD A STROLLING STORY-teller would loiter for an evening in the warmth of the ruddy fire in the great hall of some castle, beguiling the assembled guests with a tale of exploits or romance, of far places and strange peoples. The tale was told for their entertainment, and if, perchance, there was tucked deep into it some moral for those of keener perception, it lessened no whit the enjoyment of the others. Such a tale I would bring you now.

Yesterday Today

1

The Ozarks

The hart he loves the high wood,
The hare she loves the hill.

I WOULD TELL YOU A TALE OF ARKANSAS, NOT OF
the Arkansas of broad plantations of rice or cotton or strawberries; not of the Arkansas of beautiful homes, of miles upon miles of paved highways, line upon line of modern railroads; nor yet
of the Arkansas of progressive cities and towns,
with their chambers of commerce, their Rotary or
Kiwanis or Lions clubs, their consolidated schools
and state colleges. I would tell you a tale of the
Arkansas of the Ozarks, that beautiful northern
section of the state where, for great distances, even
slow trains are lacking; where from highways
branch dirt roads running back into the hills, to
become wagon tracks meandering through the
woods, and finally to dwindle to footpaths climbing to some lone cabin; of the Arkansas where
the people live as your pioneering great- or great-
great-grandparents lived; where they live as their
ancestors lived when they first isolated themselves
in these hills a hundred years ago.

Some of the things which have been written
about the Arkansas Ozark mountaineers have been
in the form of unkind wit. And often the word

"Arkansas" has been used when only remote sections of the Arkansas Ozarks were meant. Consequently, in the minds of many persons outside the state, this ridicule has attached itself not only to the people of the mountains but to the state as a whole. Many Arkansans are unable to understand how such humor was ever given credence. They know no more of isolated Ozark communities than do persons in distant places. Resenting the injustice to the Arkansas with which they are familiar, and suspecting that the mountain inhabitants are, to some degree, responsible for such stories, they have attempted to divert attention from them—to keep them from the notice of the world. Few realize that, hidden in these mountains, the state has an unique group worthy of study, protection, and, in some respects, of imitation.

Residents of the towns in the foothills of the Ozarks have seen the mountain folk who flock into town on Saturdays to do their bit of trading and then to stand in groups across the sidewalks or in the store aisles, or to sit on the stone wall around the courthouse square, visiting together. They have seen mountain men cutting wood into stove lengths in the yard behind the county relief office, wood which has been brought to town by other mountain men too proud to accept Government help without making some return. They have seen mountaineers on horseback, or in wagons, or trudging along the highway on foot, balancing a sack of flour on one shoulder and carrying another flour sack containing staple groceries or dry goods. But they have seen nothing noteworthy. Quaint terms of speech and characteristics of dress which catch the attention of a stranger have always been familiar to the townsmen and so have failed to rouse their curiosity.

Those few town dwellers who formerly lived in the hills, being even more intimately acquainted with mountain ways, do not consider them exceptional or significant.

More and more, during the summer months people from all parts of the country are following the highways into the mountains, attracted by the woods and streams and springs, for rest and fishing and hunting. But an outsider, even when his interest is caught by the hills people, has scant opportunity to know them or to see their normal home life. Most tourists do not wander far from the beaten track, and highway travel reveals little. Even trips back into the hills seldom afford an occasion for seeing more than the outsides of their houses. With a stranger for whose curiosity they cannot account they do not talk freely, and they do not share their confidences with him at all.

Perhaps it is for these reasons that more has not been told about the people of the Ozarks. Much has been written, both fact and fiction, about the inhabitants of the southern Appalachians. Their mountains were settled sooner, and they are closer to the great centers of population. Outsiders who have lived among them long enough to know them have portrayed them. The Ozark mountaineer is no less interesting than his Eastern cousin, and he is equally singular, having developed in his

own way, but we know far less about him. And
he knows no more of the outside world than that
world knows of him, for the same barriers that
have kept the world out have kept him in.

The Ozark Mountains, or highlands, appear as
uplifts in the southern part of Illinois, extend
across southern Missouri and northern Arkansas,
and disappear in Kansas and Oklahoma. They
cover a total area of about 50,000 square miles.
The transition from plain to mountain is gradual
in the north and west, but the rise of the southern
and southeastern portions, in Arkansas, is more
abrupt and rugged.

In some respects the Ozarks resemble the Alle-
ghenies, but they are much less dissected and not
so high. The main plateau region rises from 1,200
to 1,800 feet above sea level. Some points are
higher. The Bostons of Arkansas, the highest part,
reach an altitude of 2,300 feet. The average eleva-
tion of the range is about 2,000 feet.

The topography is chiefly one of ridges and
valleys cut through the limestone by the streams.
The ridges are not continuous, as in the Rocky
Mountains, but have been cut into gently rounded
peaks. These conformations are called "hills" or
"mountains," and "valleys" or "hollers" or "gaps."
One seldom hears the terms "knob" and "cove,"
which are used in the Eastern mountains.

When a traveler comes out into a comparatively
open place, with the tree-covered land rolling away
on every side, "hills" seems the proper word for the
Ozarks, but when he goes into a valley which slopes
up sharply on each side, or when he emerges sud-

Tree-covered hills

Stately black trunks

Mistletoe

denly onto some promontory with half the world
spread out at his feet, "mountain" seems more
appropriate.

These are old, old mountains—among the oldest
of the world. Slowly and surely, through the ages,
they have been worn down until now they are but
remnants of a once lofty chain.

Indications of their former grandeur are still
evident in deep gorges and rocky ravines sculp-
tured by the Arkansas and the White Rivers and
their tributaries. Water has been working underground through the ages as well, excavating enormous caverns and smaller rooms, wondrously ornamented with intricate stalactite and stalagmite
patterns of exquisite delicacy and grace.

As an aging face gains in gentleness of line as it
loses in sharpness of features, so these mountains
possess now a soft loveliness as recompense for
their loss of majestic ruggedness.

Their tops are frequently shrouded in mist. The
Indians have explained to the white man that this
is not truly mist. They say that the fairies sowed
the seeds that clothed the mountains in green.
When they had at last sown the tops of the highest
peaks they threw off their mantles and veils, which
have clung there ever since.

The rounded hills and shallow valleys are today
comfortably tree-covered, with only an occasional
peak protruding bare like the clean-shaven chin of
some giant sleeper.

There are imposing forests where beautiful old
pines raise stately black trunks thirty feet in the
air before they branch to make a thick green roof

high overhead. The ground in these groves is clear of underbrush, and the trees stand free, as in a well-kept park. The silence is heavy. A bird call cuts through the stillness like a clarion note. The more usual mountain covering is the friendly, cluttered woodland of many sorts and sizes of trees. Here are the yellow pine, the white pine, and the ash; the cedar with its little blue berries; the scaly-barked hickory, the black walnut, and the chinquapin. Beneath the trees scrub oak, huckleberry bushes, and wild hydrangeas form a thick underbrush.

In the winter the evergreens stand wide and warm in the denuded forests. Trunks of some other trees are whitish-gray, the color of cold wood ashes. Tall sweet gums, unleafed, expose the mistletoe clinging green in their topmost branches. Red berries glow among glossy holly leaves. The ground is covered with dry stalks. A form of mint has tiny dull gold bells along the stems, which tinkle faintly like wee fairy bells. Little gray snowbirds flit in and out of the bushes.

In the spring the hills are clothed in beauty. There are masses of redbud and green-tipped dogwood blossoms shimmering white in the sunshine against the faint new green which is robing the black branches of other trees in an ethereal, virescent mist. Wild honeysuckle fills the air with fragrance. Among the moss-covered rocks grow feathery ferns, wild strawberries, delicate iris like tiny orchids, phlox, geraniums, and lavender verbenas. The dry stalks on the forest floor are pushed aside by new growth. Now there is a thick carpet of

purple velvet violets. On a blue and gold April day
the gentle little brooks are lined with water cress,
which shines emerald green in the sparkling water,
and are bordered with soft spring grass sprinkled
thick with dainty lavender spring beauties and the
bright new gleam of dandelions. The birds in the
willows along the bank fill the air with their re-
joicing. A catbird mews and a mockingbird
answers and then adds a whole succession of bird-
calls, as though all the feathered folk in the forest,
one after the other, were practicing their vocal
lessons. In the early evening the birds are still.
One twitters a little, sleepily, and then awakes to
pour forth a torrent of welcoming song as the
moon, like an enormous orange, is rolled slowly up
over the horizon. Other birds join in concert. The
frogs give a nightly serenade.

On a midsummer day the woods are quiet except
for the music of a mountain brook. The crystal-
clear water of a spring bubbles up into a shallow
moss-lined pool, where it pauses for a short respite
from its play before dancing over a rock-lined run
and falling straight down the face of a bluff to
another resting pool below. At night the stillness
is broken by the plaintive wail of the mourning
dove, the repeated appeal of the whippoorwill, and
the glorious song of the mockingbird, while a
myriad fireflies twinkle.

In the fall the black gum turns crimson. Then
the oak and the hard maple blaze and the cotton-
wood is gold. Coralberry bushes are laden. The
hills are a riot of color splashed on with lavish
exuberance. The earth is covered deep with brittle

russet leaves. Persimmons and papaws are ripe.
There are nuts in abundance. Provident squirrels
are busy. Wild ducks wedge their honking way
through the sky. The haze of Indian summer is in
the air. The Indians say that Nichabo, the sun god,
has filled his great pipe and is lazily enjoying a last
smoke before he starts his long winter's nap.

The climate of the Ozarks is temperate. In the
winter there is much fog and rain, with a raw
wind, damp and chill. There is an occasional flurry
of snow. There are some days of freezing weather
and some subzero nights. Seldom is there long-
continued severe cold. Many mornings are ex-
hilarating, crisp, and clear, with the sun shining
brightly in a blue sky and the crust of the earth
frozen. By noon the earth has thawed and the air
is warm. Not until the sun is low does the cold
return.

Summer days are often oppressively hot, but
summer nights are usually cool. There are frequent rains and infrequent windstorms which may
reach destructive velocities, extracting trees as
rooted as wisdom teeth. Sometimes there is a
devastating summer drought.

Spring and fall are extended seasons of mild,
clear, beautiful weather, with days just comfortably warm and nights pleasantly cool.

Nature has been generous in the treasures which
she has hidden in the Ozarks. There are great
stores of coal, marble, granite, sandstone, and
limestone. There are rich deposits of zinc, iron,
manganese, lead, and copper. There is some silver
and a little gold. There is kaolin for making pot-

tery. There are whetstones and honestones, rock crystal and slate, phosphate rock and glass sand, onyx and precious and semiprecious stones. And there is abundant undeveloped water power.

2

A Fur Piece Through the Woods

Seesaw, Sacaradown,
Which is the way to London town?
One foot up, the other foot down,
That is the way to London town.

THE HORTONS WANTED TO FIND THEIR WAY TO A home far back in the hills, a home in Bone Cave Hollow. Early one morning they started north by automobile on a state highway that crosses the Ozarks and goes on into Missouri.

Most of the highways through the mountains are not paved but are graveled. The money which is available for paving is spent for thoroughfares close to the centers of population, where the traffic is greatest. Although Arkansas automobile licenses cost more and the gasoline tax is higher than in many states, the funds run short before the hard roads reach the hills.

Graveled highways are satisfactory when they are adequately and frequently scraped, but a heavy downpour plays havoc with them. When clouds loose their torrential burden and undulating silver sheets blot out the landscape, the water races down the road in tumbling streams, cutting troughs for itself and washing rocks from the surface to the ditches at the sides; or it stands in shirred pools in the low places. After such a rain the highway must be reworked.

When the Hortons set out on their journey into the hills they knew what township and, in a general way, what neighborhood they wished to reach.

When they had gone as far as their original instructions would take them, to the place where they were to turn off the state highway, they stopped to ask a crossroads storekeeper to direct them further. He said, "I don't rightly know as I kin tell you how to git there. Hit's ben such a long spell sence I was back there I sorter disremember. There ain't no right good way as I know of fer sartin. I have a mind to send a couple of the kids with you as fur as the Kellys', if it would please you to take 'em. They could show you that fur easier than I could tell it, and the Kellys kin tell you from there. I disremember if there's ben a car go through that-a-way clean to where you're aimin' on goin', but Doc Kelly—he's a low man with glasses. He ain't rightly no doc. That's jest his name—Doc Kelly he drives the mail route so I know you kin git that fur, and I reckon you kin git all the way to Dry Run Crick. Then it's jest a little piece down that to Bone Cave Holler." They learned later how mixed his geography was but they could not question his gracious willingness to help them.

When they protested that the children would have a long return walk, he assured them that the Kellys', though several miles by road, was "jest a little smidgen more than a mile" from the store by a path which cuts directly across the hills, and "the kids would jest as leave come back that-a-way."

Then he and his wife told the children about the way "along past the Jenkinses', around Wheelers' fur cotton patch"—and so forth.

As they started out again, the Hortons' thanks were politely acknowledge by a "Yours truly" from the storekeeper's wife and the storekeeper's briefer "Yours."

They were on a county road now, graded but not surfaced. This would get deeply rutted in a rain and need frequent regrading. They crossed a high bridge over Coon Creek, so high that it looked misplaced over the tiny stream of water in the rocky creek far below. But they guessed that in the spring that trickle might become a raging torrent which would threaten to sweep this bridge away.

They learned where old cars and tires go. They saw them standing in the yards of the houses they were passing, and they had seen some in yards along the highway. The model-T Fords have gone to the mountains. Here boys show real talent in making a five-dollar automobile run with replacements salvaged from discarded cars. An automobile cemetery, where the remains of aged cars in all stages of disintegration are abandoned, is never safe from pilfering as long as any parts are left. A worn tube and casing can be bought from a filling station for twenty-five or fifty cents, patched and booted elaborately, and used repeatedly. And who would want a good car or good tires to drive over some of these roads anyway?

Many cars are being run in the hills with license tags several years old. Recently a man drove into a county seat in a car bearing a 1912 license. When questioned, he asserted that he had understood that a new tag must be obtained only at the time when an automobile was purchased. Accordingly, he was still displaying the one he had got with his car. Ordinarily an old tag is used because there is no money for a new one.

In spite of leniency in regard to license dates, many automobiles are out of service. Occasionally replacement parts are required which cannot be found but must be bought, and money is necessary for gasoline. When cash is not available the car is left standing in the yard, with all the tires flat; and the cushions—what remains of them—are used as seats on the porch, perhaps, or on the ground under a tree.

One man explained the situation thus: "Hit was so fur to walk to town (it's a good twenty-five mile) that I reckoned I'd git me a little old rattle-trap of a car. But it wasn't much, and it's about fell to pieces, and we cain't git no money fer gas now, and we cain't sell the car exceptin' on credit, and that's jest like givin' it away, so there it sets."

The Hortons' route was leading them farther into the hills, past the Jenkinses' and the Wheelers', past Lizbeth Church House and the Poor People's Farm. They came to a creek which crossed their way, far out of sight of any habitation. It had cut too deeply to be forded by a car, so a bridge had been built. During some recent rain the water had been high and rushing here, and the flooring had been washed away. Only the two transverse logs now spanned the creek bed. These cross logs were halves of a tree trunk, eight or ten inches in diameter, split lengthwise and laid with the flat side turned up, to support the floor boards. The ends of the logs were sunk in the bank at each side, the tops nearly flush with the surface of the road. They were in line with the wheel tracks. The travelers were a long way from their destination— too far to walk—so Mrs. Horton and the children traversed the stream on foot and Mr. Horton backed and straightened the car until the wheels were aligned with the logs. Then holding the steering wheel steady, he inched the car over the creek and arrived safely on the other side.

They had left the county road now, and were following ungraded wheel tracks with grass growing between them. Lanes branched off frequently, so that the guides must continually tell the driver which fork to take. He would have little difficulty in retracing the route, for if he were in doubt as to which way to turn he would only have to ascertain which fork his tires had run on. Except for Mr. Kelly's tire tracks there were no other marks with which to confuse them now. Only wagons are used by others here.

They reached the Kellys' and their guides left them. They must go a "right smart piece through the woods in Possum Holler" and inquire again, they were told. That was to be their procedure from then on, finding their way by inquiring at the houses they passed for further information.

They learned to call Barren township "Barn," and Dota "Doty," in the interest of intelligibility. It did not take them long to learn that it was not necessary for one of them to get out of the car and go to the door of a house for directions. The throb of the engine had been heard a long way off, and someone was probably peeping out the door or window, ready to come as soon as Mr. Horton sounded the horn.

But easily as directions were got, they were not always so easily followed. They were told, "Take the second fork to the left." Then they must guess whether the dim wagon trail that wandered off into the woods was counted, or whether it was so unimportant that it had been forgotten and the two forks they were to look for were more distinct. And whichever way they decided, they might have to go for miles before being able to verify their choice. Or they might be watching for the third house on the right. Were they to count only the houses close to the road, or did one set "a half a quarter" back in a field count too?

If there had been names on the mailboxes, it would have helped them for a time, but the post-man knows everyone, so names are unnecessary, and before long they were not on a mail route anyhow.

A woman with children would tell them to go past the school. The next woman, with all her family grown, would tell them to go past the church house, and how were they to know that in this case it was one and the same building? Or, being directed to ford the creek twice, they made the mistake of counting a branch that they forded, as one of the crossings. Or they were to turn at the first plain fork or at the top of the first big hill—not the little ones, but the big one. How plain is plain, and how big is big?

One type of direction which particularly bothered them was, "Turn right on the first road this side of the big road." To follow it they must go on to the highway and then retrace their way.

But as they considered how they would direct someone in this country—someone who did not know the names of the bayous or branches or hills, who did not know the dwellers in any of the houses nor to whose home any of the byways led, who was unfamiliar with the names and locations of schools or any other landmarks—they decided that their guides were doing well to hand them along from one to the next, on a trail getting ever warmer, until at last they should reach their goal.

Their way was getting steadily worse. "You cain't git through there in no car," they were told at one house where they inquired. But their next informant was more encouraging. "Foller this road till you ford this here crick three times. Then the first house you come to you turn left around their kitchen garden and foller the lane. Hit's rough but you-all kin git through there all right if you jest take it slow."

They found that they had no choice but to "take it slow." The advice was like an old sign, warning "Speed Limit 45 miles," beside a highway under construction.

They threaded their way down a lane between fields, an uneven lane which tipped and twisted the car, a lane grown high with bushes on each side which scratched the sides of the car and snapped

A highway through the hills

On the mail route

A suspension footbridge

in the windows at their faces. They went through
gates and across fields and on into the woods
beyond.

It was indeed rough. The way had been cleared
enough for a wagon but they had to be constantly
on the watch for stumps or rocks over which a
wagon could pass, but on which the car would be
caught. Now and then, to avoid something insurmountable, Mr. Horton left the track entirely and
blazed a trail of his own under the trees, hoping
that there were no leaf-covered mudholes. After a
rain it may take a long time for a field or a level
bit of woods to dry out.

There were no longer any bridges. Sometimes
the little road forded the creek half a dozen times
in a mile. Sometimes it gave up trying to hold onto
the bank and ran along the rocky creek bed through
water so clear that it was impossible to judge the
depth correctly.

The little streams in the hills rise rapidly when
there is a heavy rain and become impassable, but
they go down again just as quickly when the rain
is over, except at flood time, when they may block
all passage for days.

In some places the road slanted precipitously. A
horse can pull a tilted wagon as long as it does not
tip entirely over, so the users wait until the stream
has washed away a really dangerous amount from
one side of the lane which skirts it before they
will bother to fill it in again.

Some of the time the road ran along the extreme
verge of a bluff. The Hortons came to places where
it did not seem possible that a car could squeeze

between a boulder or a tree and the edge. They knew that wagons went that way, but that a car never had. They could not tell whether or not a few more inches of dirt had caved off the edge or been washed away by a rain since a wagon had passed by. They looked over the brink to make sure that the last vehicle which had tried to cross this tricky-looking stretch was not at the bottom. But they discovered no casualty, so they went on.

At the next cabin where they stopped for directions, the woman deliberated. "Well, I couldn't rightly tell you," she concluded, "but me and the kids'll go along and show you if you don't care to have us."

So she and her two little ones climbed into the car.

"If you-uns jest keep a-goin' this-a-way we'll git clean to Bone Cave Holler fer sartin," she declared convincingly as she pointed down a trail that bored straight into a pine forest. She was the only real optimist they found, where the condition of the roads was in question.

Suddenly, as they went through the woods, the trail disappeared. The earth from between the wheel tracks dropped away into a rapidly deepening ravine and the tracks faded out. Mr. Horton had no choice but to back until the car was on even ground again and then to try to turn around without getting hopelessly caught between the close-grown trees.

Their guide was as surprised and disappointed as they were. "Lord!" she exclaimed, "I never did hear tell of this place." She had been enjoying the novelty of the ride and hoping that it might continue.

When she discovered that there was no more riding in store, she concluded that the Hortons could find their way unaided.

"I had ruther go back as to go on. The kids is plumb gin out," she explained. "Jest you keep to that there path and you cain't miss it," she assured them cheerfully, as she and her brood started for home. The Hortons suspected that they had never been that far afield before.

Mr. and Mrs. Horton went down the ravine, crossed a little brook on steppingstones, and started to climb up the hill on the other side, pausing now and then, when they were out of breath, to sit on some large rock to rest and look down on the lower land they had left behind. When they were high enough to see the roof of a house through the tree-tops far below, they came to another cabin.

They stopped there for further directions from a woman who had stood on the porch, watching their approach and speaking reassuringly to the dogs. She led them through the house yard and the barn lot to the edge of an old cotton field. She stayed there after pointing across to the woods on the opposite side to show them where a footpath be-gan, and explaining, "There ain't exactly no path here but you cut acrost this field and go into them woods directly you reach the fur corner." They made their way down the furrows across the field, their shoes taking on a cargo of loose dirt at every step. Following the signaled directions of their pilot, who still stood where they had left her, they at last discovered the little path that wound its way among the trees, and, waving their thanks, they again entered the woods.

Except for the faint babble of a brook, these woods were deathly quiet. Conversation seemed a sacrilege. The Hortons walked on in silence.

Soon they were climbing once more. At last they reached the top of the rise, crossed a ridge, and found themselves at the edge of a bluff overlooking a beautiful long wooded valley. Nestled in the valley was a house, with smoke curling lazily from its chimney. By this sign of the nearness of other persons the spell of silence was broken.

Remembering their directions, they kept to the top of the cliff until they reached a place where a fallen tree trunk extended from the level on which they stood to a ledge part way down the face. This was their stairway, so they scrambled and slid down its length and landed safely on the ledge fifteen feet below. They skirted this shelf until they found a footpath cut into a slightly less abrupt slope. They scrambled and slid down again until they reached the gentler grade at the foot.

When they finally arrived at their destination they were surprised to find a wagon road in front of the house but they learned that it merely ran from the barn lot to a field. People cannot get out of this valley except on foot by the way the Hortons had come, or on horseback by a very circuitous route.

After their tiring journey they welcomed the cold spring water which their friends offered them. They continued their visit as long as they dared

Watching their approach

Fording the creek

A ferryboat

A modern oxcart

without running the risk of having to make their return trip in the dark.

As they eventually attempted to find their way back, the path seemed to have grown indistinct. They had expected to retrace their steps without difficulty but soon they came to a turn where they realized that, much as all these rocks and trees looked alike, they had never seen this particular combination before. They had tried to convince themselves that the scenery seemed different only because they were going in the opposite direction to that by which they had arrived. But they were now sure that they had missed their way and they turned back. After other similar deviations they ultimately reached their car.

If their quest had led them along the river ways and across the swamps their difficulties would have been almost equally great. If there had been rain within the last week the county road, although hard and dry over most of its surface, would probably have had numerous holes full of mud and water, three feet across and several inches deep, dropped right out of the apparently solid earth. The river "bottom land" dries very slowly.

The usual swamp is a low defile running back from the river into the bottoms. It is inundated each time the level of the river rises a little, and it never drains completely after a rain. It may partly or entirely surround a higher bit of land near the river, which requires more of a rise to flood it.

To reach these higher places the Hortons would have had to cross the swamp. There is no dry land

here. There are occasional holes filled with stag-
nant water, where tadpoles, wiggle-tails, and moc-
casins abound, but most of the surface is heavy
black mud, solid enough to walk on, almost covered
with decaying black leaves. The whole swamp is
black—black trees growing thick, black mud, black
leaves, and dead black logs lying on the ground.
Even the air seems dusky and dank.

Where the surface of the mud is not solid enough
to support a person's weight, dead logs have been
laid end to end to form a path. These are a welcome
sight to the stranger, for they serve to mark the
trail. The swamp is no place for an aimless, meandering stroll.

People live in the swamps. People live in lone
valleys and on the hills surrounding them. They
live in valleys as hard to reach as the one the Hortons visited, and in another valley over the hill
beyond that, and yet others farther on; in valleys
connected with each other and with the outside
world only by footpaths. Some of the people have
never been outside their own valley. Most persons
are known no farther than three or four miles
away. It would be as difficult for many of them
to find their way out as it is for strangers to find
their way in, for they would be no more familiar
with the country they would have to cross, or with
the landmarks.

The people in the mountains farther east, although having the same ancestors, nevertheless
differ from the mountaineers of the Ozarks, because, in their separate isolations, they have developed their own variations of their common heri-

tage. So, to a lesser degree, the people in one Ozark valley may differ from those in another in speech, custom, or belief.

Rivers, as well as mountains, serve as barriers. There are few bridges across the large rivers in the mountains. Instead, at infrequent intervals, there are ferries. The ferry crossing is located at a place where the bank on each side is high. A cable is stretched from one bank to the other. The ferryboat is a flatboat large enough to accommodate two or three team-drawn wagons. It is connected, by pulley, to an overhead cable and propelled by a small motorboat fastened alongside. A fee is charged for passage.

Some of the people have not been beyond their immediate neighborhood for years. Some, within twenty bad mountain miles of a town, have never been there. Great numbers have never seen a train, many have never ridden in an automobile, and some have never seen one. For many persons the only means of travel is on foot.

In sections farthest from good roads oxen are still used to draw wagons. Only they are strong enough to pull heavy loads through the mud and deep sand of the worst mountain trails.

Though a family owns a horse it may be necessary to conserve for the work at home all the strength the animal can glean from scant rations, and unnecessary jaunts are dispensed with.

Most men who own a wagon make at least an annual trip to town. But the wagon may be loaded high with cotton on the way in, and with a winter's supply of provisions on the way home, so that, year

after year, there is never any room for the women-
folk.

Then, too, a twenty-mile trip with a loaded wagon
over mountain roads is often a six-hour drive.
Time must be allowed in town for taking a sample
of cotton up and down Main Street, to be pulled out
and tested by the cotton buyers standing on the
street corners, for a man wants to find the highest
bidder. After the cotton is sold and paid for, the
farmer must do his year's trading at the stores.
Altogether, this means that the journey must start
hours before daylight and end long after dark, and
someone must stay at home to do the milking and
"swill the pigs."

Persons who live near a town, or who have
cars, may go in every week or two, even though
only to visit, but to many others this trip is the
experience of a lifetime. To more, it is not a desirable thing. Why would they want to leave home?
Everything for which they care is there. Neither
the idea of getting into unfamiliar surroundings
nor of rubbing shoulders with "furriners" is appealing. The lack of some material thing or the
necessity of disposing of their produce may take
them out of their hills for a little time, but their
contact with the surrounding world creates in most
of them no desire to prolong that contact. Like
many other peoples, they are provincially self-satisfied and self-sufficient. Their ways seem right to
them, and other ways seem queer.

3

Architecture

Knock at the door!
Draw the latch!
And walk in!

ARCHITECTURE, ACCORDING TO WEBSTER, IS THE ART
or science of building. As the word has come to
connote science, and brings to mind imposing struc-
tures, it is inappropriate to Ozark mountain homes,
for they are neither imposing nor scientifically
built. Insofar as it implies art it is permissible,
for there is an unconscious art about many of them
that is most picturesque.

A house of brick or painted boards is congruous
in cleared and cultivated fields, but it is a jarring
note in a forest setting, while a house of logs or of
richly colored native stone fits the background as
though it had grown there.

Mountaineers do not have brick homes and seldom do they build of stone. Houses that they build
on the highways, aping civilization, may be of
planed boards. Left unpainted, or with an original
coat of paint peeling off, they are extremely unat-
tractive. But the cabins deep in the mountains are
of logs.

A new log house is a pretty sight, with the soft
gold of its stripped logs and shingles gleaming

through the trees. No less artistic is the old home
of weathered logs, set in the midst of beauty, on a
hill which falls away from the front of the house
and rises obliquely behind, with projections of copper-colored rock showing here and there through
the green foliage.

Minnie Cannon and her first husband, Bill, had
been most atypical mountaineers, in that they had
the wanderlust. Soon after their marriage they
had got an old model-T touring car. With all the
necessities of life piled into the back seat, or tied
on to the automobile somewhere, they had set out to
see the world. When they ran out of money they
would find work wherever they happened to be and
stay until they had earned enough to enable them
to move on. They might have gone on indefinitely
had not Minnie "heired a good place from her pa."
Upon receiving the news, they returned to the
mountains to settle down.

Bill died and Minnie married again. When the
second husband proved shiftless, she "run him off."
"As long as I was a-havin' to tend to things by my
own self anyhow, there warn't no reason to have a
good-fer-nothin' man hangin' around jest a-wait-
in' fer his vittles." She had no children.

Although tethered by her property, Minnie
would often give vent to her desire to roam by
visiting her neighbors. She had friends far outside
the limits of her own community. She would take
a coffeepot so that at noon she could build a little
fire in some pretty spot near the road and make
coffee to drink with the lunch she had brought.

Her cousin, Ruth Cannon, a "furriner" to the

mountains, came to visit her. Ruth expressed an interest in mountain houses, and Minnie, welcoming an opportunity for a trip, offered to take her to see some. She was a fine guide because, being familiar with the world "outside," she knew what things were peculiar to the hills.

On the day on which they were to make their calls, Ruth arose early, according to her calculation, but Minnie had been up and working since daybreak and was ready for a second breakfast.

The coffee had been simmering on the back of the stove for hours. She threw into the pot the thin white lining from eggshells to settle the grounds. As she outlined her plans for the day, they sat at her oilcloth-covered table and ate cold biscuits as big as saucers, spread with delicious, tart wild muscadine jelly, and drank coffee as bitter as medicine and thick toward the bottom of the cup.

The first house they were to visit was "yon side o' Coon Crick." They drove as far as they could in Ruth's car and then followed a dim footpath through the leafless winter woods.

"We gotta cross a log to git there, but the crick's real small," Minnie assured Ruth.

Their path ended suddenly at the creek and they were brought up short. Instead of a harmless little brook, they saw a stream fully twenty feet wide, and it looked deep. Instead of one log across it, there were two, one small one from the shore to the roots of an overturned and partly submerged tree stump near the side on which they stood, and another large log, fully three feet thick, extending from the stump to the opposite bank.

"Well, good land! There warn't nothin' like this the last time I was by this-a-way," Minnie exclaimed in surprise.

Ruth set foot on the small log gingerly. It turned. She stopped, deterred by the thought that it would be many miles back to dry clothing. Minnie considered the feasibility of crawling along the log to the stump, and touched it tentatively. It turned again.

As they stood back, deliberating, they heard a "Hello" from across the creek and up the hill, and discerned something moving toward them through the trees. It proved to be their prospective host, Uncle Henry Martin, coming to the rescue. He came across to them without difficulty, balancing easily on the swaying log, and soon found more logs to bridge the distance to the stump, and placed them securely.

He explained that the water had been dammed up here till it was at least eight feet deep, to make a good fishing hole near home. Why this particular spot had been chosen for the dam, or why, when it was chosen, the family bridge had not been moved, was a mystery. It was probably simpler to leave it as it was and let the family learn to balance.

Aunt Nancy Martin was washing, using a stick to stir the clothes as they boiled in a big black iron kettle set over a bonfire in the yard. Much of her washing was already complete. The clothes were hung on the fence or spread out on bushes to dry. She hastily scraped the coals from under the kettle and invited Ruth and Minnie into the house.

Having turned the guests over to Aunt Nancy,

Uncle Henry said no more. Mountain men usually let the women do the talking to other women.

Before they accepted Aunt Nancy's invitation, Minnie called Ruth's attention to the outside of her home. It was a fine example of old Southern architecture, with the two rooms set apart, with an open hallway between, a porch, or "gallery," clear across the front, and one roof over all.

In the warm South, houses were built with these open passageways through the center in order to catch every breeze that stirred, and to offer refuge from the heat. When Southerners came to the Ozarks they built their homes in the style to which they had been accustomed, that is, with the opening called the "dog trot," "dog run," "dog alley," "wind sweep," or simply "passage." But the Arkansas mountain breezes are not all hot, so, gradually, walls and doors are being put over the ends of these passages, for the winter at least, to furnish a sheltered way between the two living rooms of the house. But the Martins' house still stands as it was originally built.

"The roof is all over shingles or shakes rived by hand with a froe," Minnie explained. The ridge was finished in true Ozark style, by the simple expedient of extending the shingles from one side of the roof beyond the ridge, letting them jut out into space. The walls were of logs. At one end was a great gray stone chimney.

The floor of the room with the fireplace was close to the ground, but as the house was built on a hill, the walls at the other end were supported on piles of flat stones, stacked without mortar. One end of the porch floor rested on the ground. The distance up to the other end was broken by a keg, set up as a step.

Having completed their inspection of the outside of the house, they accepted Aunt Nancy's invitation to go in.

"Won't you pull off your hats?" she requested hospitably as they entered the room to the left of the gallery.

The large fireplace of native field stone was the outstanding thing about this room. It occupied half of the end wall. Great logs were burning there. A soot-blackened kettle hung from a crane over the coals. In it beans and salt pork were simmering. The hearth in front of the fire was also of stone. It had cracked and sunk two or three inches in the middle, until the stones rested on the ground.

The life of a mountain family centers about the fireplace in any house that has one. The chairs are drawn up to it. The beds are in the same room. Much of the cooking is done there, and the sadirons are heated on the hearth.

It is not only the source of heat but also of light on dark winter evenings (evening is any time between noon and sundown), and at night. It furnishes a pleasant light by which to sit and visit after dark before the early bedtime.

When additional light is needed, a coal-oil lamp may be used. A family may burn no more than a gallon of oil in the lamps in a year. Some people still make hand-dipped candles. Aunt Nancy showed Ruth her old candle molds and explained their use. The lack of brighter artificial light is not

The passage

Scalding the clothes

A modern box house

A typical ridge line

Farm Security Administration photograph by Shahn

A plate and a bowl

Farm Security Administration photograph by Shahn

A well-chinked house

considered a great misfortune. During the farming season the people are so tired that they drop right into bed when the day's work is done, and in the winter most reading or sewing can be done by daylight.

It was surprising that candles could be kept lighted in that room. The chinking had come out from between many of the logs. Some of the cracks had been stuffed with rags and paper to help keep out the wind, but there were still plenty of spaces for drafts.

In this room were two beds, some chairs, an old bureau, a small table, and a trunk. One of the beds was an ornate iron one which had originally had a coat of white enamel. The other was a beautiful Jenny Lind. The bureau was a fine old walnut piece, heavily ornamented with hand carving that gleamed in the firelight with a soft rich luster.

There are no closets in these cabins. Any surplus clothing is hung from pegs or folded away in drawers or in a trunk. Above the puncheon door (made of hand-split slabs) was the ever-present gun, supported on pegs. On the wall over one of the beds hung a guitar. A ladder was nailed to one wall of the room, leading to an opening through the ceiling into the loft above.

Aunt Nancy took them into the room across the passage. Here was a kitchen table at which meals were both prepared and eaten. Chairs were brought in from the other room at mealtime. In few mountain homes are there enough chairs for the whole family. The more rapidly the family increases, the more difficult it is to buy additional furniture, and beds are more necessary than chairs.

Under the table stood a large can for corn meal. Another container, the flour can, was covered with the mixing board. A wooden chest was set against the wall. When there is no smokehouse, or when it is full, salt meat is kept in such a chest in the house. In one corner was a small cookstove. Some cooking and baking could be done more conveniently here than in the fireplace.

There was an old-fashioned safe, its zinc-covered doors ornamented with punched designs. Here the utensils and the staple groceries were kept. A mountain woman ordinarily puts salt, baking powder, and other small-quantity groceries into clear glass jars. Almost invariably she will take the top from the jar to show how much is inside.

Cooking utensils are usually scarce in these cabins. A black pot, a frying pan, and a bucket are fair equipment. The family which can also boast a bread pan, a piepan, and a dishpan is indeed fortunate. Tableware is likewise simple. A *set* of dishes is almost unheard of. A plate, a cup, and a bowl apiece are ample, and the bowl can be dispensed with. There is no silverware. Steel forks, knives, and spoons suffice.

Through the spaces between the floor boards of this room chickens could be seen scratching for crumbs under the house.

In answer to Ruth's question about the age of her home Aunt Nancy said, "I don't rightly know, exactly. Hit's somewhars over a hundred year old, I reckon. I was borned here, the youngest of fifteen, and my paw was borned here, and his pappy afore him. My great-gran'pappy raised it when he wedded my great-gran'maw and brung her here from acrost the mountains."

Minnie reminded Ruth that if they were to visit the other homes which she had arranged for her to see, they must be on their way.

As they took their leave, Aunt Nancy stood on the porch to watch them, while Uncle Henry escorted them safely back over Coon Creek.

They were on their way again. "Take the right turn at the next fork," Minnie directed. "Hit's a mite further to Richardson's by that-a-way, but I want to show you somethin'."

As they were passing a group of buildings Minnie pointed. "See that shaggy barn roof a-settin' smack dab on the ground. The walls fell down in a big wind once and they've jest let it set there ever sence. And would you believe it, there's folks a-livin' under there! Hit jest goes to show it don't pay to be too nice without considerin' considerable. The young Smiths, them as is livin' there, had their house ketch fire and burn down soon after they was married. Hit was winter time, and a-rainin', and they ast Virgil Langston to give 'em leave to move their stuff in under that roof fer two-three weeks till they could git 'em another house. He's a soft-hearted feller and he let 'em do it. There ain't no windows, but the gable ends is so full of holes and there's so many leaks in the roof that they'd ought to git light and air a-plenty, and water too, come rain.

"I'm tellin' you the truth, they ben there goin' on four year a'ready, an' Virgil he cain't git shet of 'em. Their kids break down the fences, and them and their chickens tear around the garden patch till it jest ain't no use a-tryin' to plant nothin' 'cause it'll jest be ruint anyhow, Virgil says.

"And that young Mis' Smith jest sets there and says, 'This house ain't fitten to stay in. Hit's all a-goin' to rack. But it's better'n stayin' out of doors.'

"Look it! There's young Smith a-settin' there by that draggin' yard gate, and his woodpile that measley! Hit do beat me. Hit don't make sense somehow. Gid Smith, that's young Smith's pappy, he was a good man. And young Smith's a-triflin', worthless banty-shanty. Hit seems like after the old folks is laid out the young sprouts gits dilatory and do-less," she philosophized.

This long speech was actually broken up by comments on Ruth's part—a word of acknowledgment or a question, to start the flow again. Mountaineers do not make long consecutive statements.

Tom Richardson lived in a new log cabin deep in a wood, with the county roadway and Mrs. Richardson's kitchen garden the only cleared land within sight of the house. There is a kitchen garden near almost every house. This vegetable garden is ordinarily the woman's responsibility. The man breaks the ground for her in January or early February and the rest of the accomplishment and glory is hers. She plans the use of the land, saves seed, exchanges seeds and plants with her neighbors, and she and her children plant and tend and gather the produce.

The newer houses, such as Tom Richardson's,

Sorghum mill and boiling vat

Fenced house yard and kitchen garden

The latchstring is out

Butchering frame in the foreground

The storm cellar

are usually built together, without a "dog trot" separating the rooms. Except for the upstairs window and the neatly finished ridge line, the "Log Cabin Syrup" can illustrates this typical newer abode. Tom's house had a gallery across the front.

The whole place was pervaded with the atmosphere of order and loving care. Within the neatly fenced house yard were symmetrically arranged flower beds bordered with old automobile casings. From the edge of the porch roof, each supported by three wires, hung buckets and cans, which would bear a variety of foliage plants and flowering plants dripping over with bloom, when warm weather should come. From the porch roof hung a homemade porch swing. There were two comfortable-looking rocking chairs on the porch, fashioned of saplings, the seats padded with pillows.

The only living things in sight were two hens setting in a straw-lined box on a bench by the door.

As Minnie and Ruth drew close to the house a dog appeared from some place to bark at them. There are always dogs to greet visitors, commonly lean hound dogs or silky shepherd puppies. After some preliminary barking and snapping, to which they failed to retaliate, this dog judged the cousins to be harmless and allowed them to stay without further molestation. He kept right at their heels to make sure they got into no mischief but he condescendingly let Minnie pat him, and really grew quite friendly before she left.

A mule came out of the woods, scrutinized them from across the fence, saw enough, and went away.

But it was evident that there were no people

about. The door was closed, and doors are practically never closed except in extremely cold, or very stormy weather. Fuel is abundant. The side a person turns toward the fire will be hot and the other side will be cold on a cold day whether the door be open or shut; and a way is needed for smoke to get out and light to get into the room. So a closed door ordinarily means that the family is out.

In this case there was a double check, for the latchstring was out. Yes, latchstrings are still in use, as they were in the days of Mother Goose, but there is usually no latch. On the inside of the door, which is homemade, a nail is run through a spool to make a doorknob. Beside this knob is a hole through the door. A string or a strip of cloth is tied around the nail and run through the hole. When the family goes out, the door is pulled closed and fastened by wrapping the string around a nail in the outside doorframe. This is in no way a lock, of course; only a means of holding a latchless door closed. Many doors are fitted with a wooden bar which can be used to secure them from the inside, but this is of no use when there is no one in the house to lower and raise it.

As there was no one at home to talk to, the two women walked around the yard. At the side of the house was a sorghum mill for mashing the juice from the sorghum cane in the fall. There was one shed which aroused Ruth's curiosity. Under a roof supported on tall posts was a long galvanized iron trough set on a foundation of stones, with a chimney going up from one end and out through the roof. An opening in the foundation at the opposite end from the chimney was obviously for feeding fuel for a fire under the vat. Minnie was much amused at Ruth's suspicion that it might be intended for making "moonshine" liquor, and assured her that it was a boiler for boiling down the sorghum juice into molasses.

Near the back door was a smokehouse. A fine cold morning is chosen for butchering. The meat is cut up and dressed on long makeshift tables set up in the yard back of the house. The task must be done quickly, for the meat must be salted before the day becomes too warm, or it will spoil. In order to expedite the work, a number of neighbors are invited in to lend a hand; the men to help with the butchering and the women to help "render out the lard," serve dinner, and visit. Each takes home some of the fresh meat at the end of the day.

The rest of the meat is packed in thick salt and stored on shelves in the smokehouse or in chests. It is left in the salt for about six weeks. Then it may be washed in borax water or sprinkled with borax and pepper and hung from the smokehouse rafters, where it will be flavored with the fragrant smoke from burning hickory chips or sassafras.

In one corner of the yard was the storm cellar. Even the newest, sturdiest houses have their storm cellars near by, for treacherous tornadoes come suddenly in these mountains, taking everything in their path and leaving death and destruction behind. The underground cave is the only safe refuge. On summer days which are sultry and oppressive and ominously quiet, parents go about their tasks listening apprehensively for a roar like the rush of a great flood, and watching the sky for the first sign of the terrifying copper-colored funnel which presages the approach of a twister. Thus they may have time to gather the whole family to the safety of the cave under the mound of earth which marks the storm cellar before the wind may chance to swoop down on their little spot of land.

The storm cellar often serves a double purpose. This cool, damp earthen chamber may be lined with shelves for the storage of canned fruits and vegetables.

Besides the smokehouse there was one other outhouse in the yard, the toilet, set near the back fence. This was a small square frame, with three walls and no roof—just a screen offering a semblance of privacy. The family must have known from which direction to expect neighbors before deciding upon the facing of the open side. But these three walls afforded more protection than many households have.

By a provision originating with the Civil Works Administration, the Government has been building "modern" sanitary toilets for anyone who can pay the cost of materials, at the rate of one dollar a month. Some persons in Ozark towns have taken advantage of this offer, but it has affected few real mountain families. Almost none of the homes have pit toilets. Most of the toilets are surface type and unscreened and set in the most convenient place without regard to, or knowledge of, the effect on the water supply. There are still many homes without any.

Beside the large flat stone which served as a back

doorstep was a bench with a bucket of water and a washpan. The water must have come from the well near by, in which buckets were tied at the ends of a rope run over a pulley wheel which hung from the little roof over the well. The washpan is customarily kept near the front door.

Minnie and Ruth had completed their circuit of the house and were starting back toward the car when they heard voices and saw Mrs. Richardson emerging from the wood, trailing her clouds of glory behind her, seven of them, and the eighth she carried in her arms. The oldest child was ten years of age. They had all gone out early to gather poke greens. They had been deep in the woods when the dog's bark brought them scurrying home as fast as the toddlers and their mother could go. One of her feet was normal but the other was badly deformed, so that she had to hobble along.

She noticed one of the little tots running toward the end of the house. "Come back here, Novella," she called. "These here ladies won't do you no hurt. She's all the time ashamed [bashful] afore strangers, that one," she explained. "She's like to crawl back up under the floor like a hound dog."

She was very sorry that her callers had been made to wait and hurried them into the house.

There is no cold quite so cold as the clammy, penetrating frigidity of a house that has been shut up with no heat in it. The air is raw, the furniture is icy, there is no comfort anywhere. But in these cabins there is no plumbing to freeze, and it is unsafe to leave a fire in an unoccupied house. A burning log may fall apart with a shower of sparks

which can do quick damage. So the fire is smother-
ed out under ashes before the family all go away.

Their hostess offered them chairs, very cold
rockers, while she set about making a fire. In a few
moments the edge was gone from the air and Ruth
could relax a little and loosen her heavy coat, and
Minnie her lighter one. These others, without
wraps, seemed not to notice the chill. They were
accustomed to it.

Mrs. Richardson apologized for the condition of
her house. There was no evident reason for
apology, but the women with the tidiest houses are
the most likely to call regretful attention to some
bit of disorder of which they are aware. The house
seemed immaculate. The bare board floors were
scrubbed white with ashes. The beds were neatly
made and covered with hand-embroidered spreads.
Over the upper parts of the shadeless and uncur-
tained windows were tacked strips of cardboard
cut to simulate scalloped valances, an idea of deco-
ration gleaned, perhaps, from a mail-order catalog.
And—*mirabile dictu*—there was glass in both
windows!

There are very few houses that do not have at
least one pane of glass broken out and the opening
stuffed with a pillow or rag or sack, or hung over
with corrugated paper or a piece of blanket or tin.
Occasionally a broken window has a keg stuck in it.
One grows accustomed to appreciating the origi-
nality and ingenuity of families in finding coverings or stuffings for broken windows, but to find
one actually completely filled with glass is indeed
a novelty.

The walls were neatly covered with building paper which would fade in time to an ugly brown, but which was still an attractive blue. There were no joists for a ceiling, but the rafters were bridged with the corrugated paper of used packing boxes, studded with nails run through soda-pop bottle caps, probably to keep the paper from pulling over the nail heads, as well as to add ornamentation. The family must have had a storekeeper friend. One could find entertainment in that house by the hour, estimating the number of Coca Cola tops in proportion to the orange pop or the grape soda.

When the fire was burning well Mrs. Richardson availed herself of the opportunity to nurse the baby, while she was having to sit down anyway.

The other children sat on their haunches or leaned against the wall by the fireplace, one foot resting on the other, and stared at their visitors, as quiet as mice. There was little attempt to "show off" among them. They were too engrossed in watching the show. This visit would be the chief topic of conversation for a long time to come. Impressions of Ruth's appearance, dress, and manners would be exchanged with the neighbors.

She spoke of her appreciation of the house.

"I'm right proud you like it," the mistress beamed. "We lost one by fire and another by wind, and this one we've built on credit, fer we had to have shelter over us."

There would be more old houses in the hills were it not for fire. Fires are frequent and so destructive that fire insurance cannot be purchased in most parts of the mountains. A spark from a chimney, blown onto a dry roof on a windy day, can make short work of a house. It is practically impossible, with no equipment but buckets of water drawn from a well, to put out a blaze that has caught dry, unpainted shingles and logs.

Ordinarily the only real flue is the stone chimney from the fireplace. When the more modern cook-stove is added in the other room the tin stovepipe is run out through the roof or wall. When a big fire roars in the stove this pipe may get red hot. The walls may be papered with old newspapers or magazine pages. These get yellow and dry with age so that a hot pipe can make them burst into flame without warning, and the house is gone, often without time to carry out the beds.

On a table there was a small phonograph in a varnished oak case, with a few records lying on the shelf below.

"We bought that talkin' machine secondhanded from the Masseys," Mrs. Richardson explained. "We set a powerful store by music, seems like. Used to be, a young feller'd come around here and hold a singin' school, come winter. Everybody'd go, and pay him with what they had, money or foodstuffs or maybe board him while he was here. But sense times got so hard and folks is jest a-scrimpin' and a-scrabbin' by and a-livin' like porpors [paupers], he's quit comin'."

Music is highly esteemed by the mountaineers. There are community sings and singing schools. Most homes have some sort of musical instrument. A very few boast old-fashioned organs. In some neighborhoods almost every cabin has a guitar

A pillow-filled window

The well and well house

Farm Security Administration photograph by Shahn

Dry paper near the stove

Farm Security Administration photograph by Rothstein

Making yarn

A fence of pales

A stock-law gate   Kettle for hominy, soap, or clothes

hanging on the wall. In others there are fiddles, and in still others portable phonographs.

The phonograph records are almost always vocal selections. One favorite is a ditty about "Ten-Cent Cotton, Forty Cent Meat." Beautiful old songs like "Silver Threads Among the Gold" and "The Old Rugged Cross" are rendered in a murderous nasal twang. From these records the musical standards of many of the hillpeople have been derived. But you cannot get Flagstad or Melchior for a dime.

There are some radios. But there is no electricity, and many families cannot afford the original cost or the upkeep of a battery set.

The baby, who had dozed off as Mrs. Richardson talked, woke with a start, as from a bad dream, and began to whimper. His mother laid him on a bed and shuffled into the other room to make a sugar tit to soothe him. She wrapped a little sugar in a clean white cloth and tied it with a long string. The string was a retriever.

She brought it back to the howling baby, who hushed instantly to open his mouth as she touched the pacifier to his lips with a "Here it is, God bless it!" and then added, "Hit don't seem to matter how many kids a body has, you wouldn't give 'em up, once they're here."

She came back to her chair, leaving the contented baby on the bed.

There is seldom a cradle for the "little un." Floor space is at a premium, and the baby is still a baby when he must make room for the next addition to the family anyway. The one-year-old and the new baby sleep with their parents. The other children sleep together in a second bed until it becomes too crowded. Then a third is added.

Ruth asked about something which was hanging overhead. It proved to be a quilt frame suspended by ropes in such a way that it might be let down when in use and drawn up out of the way the rest of the time. Her hostess lowered it to show her the quilt she was making. She had made the top of colored scraps left from her sewing, pieced together with plain patches from salt and tobacco sacks.

"We ben usin' some of Tom's mother's quilts sence our fire, but she's a-comin' fer 'em as quick as ever it fairs up, so I gotta git me some made. I got tops enough pieced fer us, and I got cotton laid by fer fillin' but I hain't got no more linin's." Muslin for linings takes money.

Aside from the money value, it is especially hard for a woman to lose quilts in a fire. She had made them herself and she knows the history of each scrap that goes into them, so that her quilts seem like a part of her.

"As soon as ever I git quilts enough fer us I orter start on 'em fer the kids." A good mountain mother begins to make them for her children when they are tiny. She hopes, as each daughter marries, to be able to give her ten or twelve quilts, a feather bed, and two pillows. A girl usually is given a trunk, too.

She showed the cards with which she carded the cotton for her quilts. They were a pair of boards about five inches wide by ten inches long, with spikes set into them in rows, like a steel-bristled brush. Across the backs were leather straps under which she slipped her hands. With one on each hand, she combed out the cotton between them until all the fibers lay parallel to one another and were soft and free of extraneous matter. Wool is carded in the same way in the hills. Then it is made into yarn on old spinning wheels. The yarn is dyed and knitted into socks and shawls and other things.

The sun was high overhead when the cousins left the Richardsons'. They stopped in a little clearing in the woods to eat their lunch. There stood an old stone chimney. The house must have burned down long ago, for it was all gone, but the outline of the old porch was marked by a row of jonquils blooming there. Some woman had planted the bulbs around her "home place," and each year they continued to send forth their messengers again to tell the world that it was spring, though no one was there to see; and to proclaim staunchly that love of beauty and pride in home once dwelt there, though they were gone long since.

Minnie told Ruth something of the next house they were to visit. "Hit's different from them we've seen. These are real pore folks. Jim Cossey, he's a right goodhearted, happy-go-lucky feller who wouldn't work much if he had a chance. Truth to tell, he ain't worth shootin' and he ain't got nothin' but a woman and a passel of kids, and all on starvation.

"If you want to see a real nice house sometime, go to Homer Ramsey's. I don't know 'em so I cain't take you there but I've heerd tell as it's a sight better'n most."

Fences are interesting. The kitchen garden is fenced with hand-cut pickets placed contiguously around the field to keep out the chickens and pigs. Most fences seem to be built to keep things out rather than in.

Yards may be fenced with wire or with pales. The reason for fencing house yards is not evident, for there are usually chickens on both sides and going over and under the fence.

Fields must be fenced to protect the crop from the livestock—one's own or one's neighbor's. Lack of fencing has been responsible for many a ruined crop or garden. A field may be surrounded with a wire or a zigzag rail fence.

To prevent animals from straying beyond reclaim, some sections, comprising many farms, are completely surrounded by fence. Where these stock-law fences cross a highway, a stock-law gate is built, with a cattle guard of boards set in the road in such a manner that animals cannot cross where the fence is discontinued to provide unobstructed transit for cars. There is a gate in the fence near by for teams to pass through. Only on highways are these openings for motor vehicles required. On any less important road the automobile driver, like the teamster, must still open the gate before him and close it after his car has gone through. On many Ozark highways it is not safe to drive fast at night, for just ahead or around the next curve a mule or a cow may be sleeping in the road.

Stock-law fences must be maintained, but there is no law requiring a man to care for his own fences. To reach the Cosseys' it was necessary to cross three fields and go through three gates. Made of heavy timbers, they were sagging gates which dragged the ground. It took all of Minnie's strength to open them.

Finally they got as far as the Cosseys' fence. There was probably a gate in that fence somewhere, but not where they met it. Some fences have stiles, or at least boards nailed flat between the posts, one above the other, to facilitate the crossing. Some have a stump placed on end on each side of the fence, high enough to enable a person to step from one to the other over the wire. But this fence had no manner of help, not even a hole through it, so they had no choice but to scramble over.

Their first view of Mrs. Cossey was of a wide spread of hips as she bent over an open kettle in the yard, making strong brown soap of suet and lye. The kettle was the one she also used for making hominy, and for "scalding" clothes on washday. She straightened as they drew nearer and came to greet them.

Her home was a miserable little cabin of one room and a lean-to. It had been built with a door and two windows in the room, but windows and front door were gone—possible carried off to complete another house at some time when this one had stood vacant—and only the frames were left.

The doorway was so low that it was necessary for the women to stoop as they stepped over the sill onto the dirt floor of the room.

The fire was smoking profusely. Their eyes

smarted and watered until they could scarcely see. They were glad enough that the door and windows were missing.

As they grew accustomed to the smoke they were able to look around more easily. Everything seemed to be a uniform dirty gray, both the covers on the beds and the clothing on the people. Several hens perched on one bed seemed not to mind the hue. Mrs. Cossey had one of the children shoo them out when her guests went in, but they soon returned.

There was a terrible odor in the house. Someone had had an altercation with a skunk. It was obvious why the stench was so intense. The animal's skin was stretched out to dry on the wall above the fireplace.

Two walls of the room were covered with old newspapers to keep the wind from whistling through. One wall was partly papered with wallpaper samples. The patchwork effect was interesting. As she is able to get more sample books, Mrs. Cossey will gradually get her cabin walls all papered that way. But in the meantime, as the women entered, one boy was busily engaged in flattening used packing boxes and fastening them over some of the worst cracks.

From the joists overhead hung bunches of peppers, and tobacco leaves and ears of corn also dried there.

The house had the usual ill-assorted collection of furniture, but with one startling difference. All the pieces had been given a coat of vivid orchid paint, even to a lard can which was used as a seat, and it was all dirty. The effect was that of brightly enameled fingernails which need cleaning. One thing had escaped the paintbrush. It was a heavy beveled plate-glass mirror in a wide frame of dark wood.

Jim Cossey was lying on one of the beds. He made no effort to rise. "I got the malarial fever and I'm a-chillin' and fevered today," he excused himself.

Under him there was neither mattress nor springs. There was only a feather bed partially covering the slats. Over him was a quilt. He had followed Ruth's glance.

"We aim to have a mattress when we kin git a-holt of some tickin'. Our neighbor next down has promised some straw to stuff it with. That's not so bumpy as corn shucks. Or we might git us some cotton from the Relief Office. We ain't got no sheets, neither." Usually there is at least one pair of sheets to a bed, though often there is no change.

"I suspicion we hadn't orter be livin' here by rights," he observed. "We got put off of the place where we was a-livin' and we didn't have nowheres else to go. We'd heerd about this here little place, but the feller what owns it lives in Oklyhomy."

Mrs. Cossey carried on. "One of our big girls writ him a letter. (We got us some married kids strung around hereabouts. I wish they was here so you-all could come to know 'em.) She writ, fer Jim he was too backward to ax, but we never got no answer, so we jest come on and moved in. I hope he won't run us off if he ever takes a notion to come back."

"Who owns the house?" Ruth asked.

Mrs. Cossey stepped over to the wall and read the name of the owner from an address label on one of the newspapers there.

They discussed building problems with Mr. Cossey. "A body kin build a house like this fer five dollar if he has wood on his own place," he told them. "He kin cut his own logs and split his own shingles, but he has to buy the nails and windows and the smoothed boards fer the doorframes."

"You have plenty of trees around here. Why don't you put a floor in the house?" Ruth inquired.

"You cain't well floor a house with puncheons you split your own self," he explained. "They're too rough, and if I taken 'em to the mill to git 'em planed it would cost me. Someday I reckon I'll do it."

A hen on one of the beds began to cackle loudly and rose proudly to disclose a newly laid egg.

Mr. Cossey hurried on. "Sometime I aim to put on another room, if we stay here. We shore are crowded in. The least one sleeps with her maw and me nights, and that's all right, but the other five's gittin' so that space is plumb skeerce in the other bed. The oldest boy here's thirteen."

It is hard to understand the crowding of the mountain family—congestion as extreme as would be found in the worst New York slum, as far as the living space for a single family is concerned. Land and logs are plentiful, and yet the usual mountain house has only one or two rooms. Occasionally a lean-to is added, or the loft may be utilized, if there is one. There are some four-room houses, but they are not typical. Often the houses are filled with furnishings till there is hardly room to move around. Even the stock is crowded or left without shelter. Barns in the hills would be sheds in many farming districts.

The number of rooms is surely not limited for the sake of effecting heating economy, for there is wood in abundance. Of course it requires time and effort to cut it and get it to the house. Perhaps the trouble *is* with the price of nails. Or perhaps it is that pioneer ancestors built only one or two rooms —in their case because they were pressed for time in this wilderness where food was more difficult to gain than shelter—and their descendants have stuck to the original pattern.

There can be no semblance of privacy when a family lives together in such cramped quarters.

But mountaineers still have one advantage over the slum dwellers. Neighbors are not so near. In many places less congested than New York City, houses are so close together that you can set your watch by the time signal on your neighbor's radio. The mountaineer does not have neighbors that close. If he had, they would probably not have a radio. And if they did, he would not have a watch.

Mrs. Cossey seemed to feel that some explanation of the condition of the house was in order. "Everything is as dirty as a pigpen. But the well rope's broke, and we have to tote water such a fur piece we're right sparin' of it. And I jest ben a-draggin' around." She leaned closer. "I'm a-lookin' to flop up in the bed most any time now."

No one carries water for drinking and washing and cooking and bathing for the joy of the carrying. Numbers of these people have perpetually running streams on their own land, with a sufficient fall to be piped to a kitchen sink and a bathroom. Others have wells or springs near by, from which water could be pumped into storage tanks higher than the house. But they do not avail themselves of this convenience because they are not aware of the possibility. Few even have pumps in their wells. They continue to carry water from the nearest source. If their own well becomes polluted they will go to a neighbor's. If there is a drouth and their water source dries up, they may have to put barrels and buckets in the wagon and drive for miles to some spring or stream that is still flowing.

Minnie asked if Ruth might see the kitchen.

"Johnnie, you-all go skeer the pig out of there afore the lady come," Mrs. Cossey directed.

They got there just in time to see the last of the pig disappearing through the doorway.

The door between the main room and the lean-to had been closed, and the outside door of this kitchen had been standing open. Across one end of the lean-to was a partition about two feet high and three feet out from the wall. The bin thus made was filled with unhusked corn and cornstalks. The pig was evidently allowed free access. There were no outbuildings of any sort.

There was no window in this room. The door was left open in the daytime.

An old laundry stove without any oven was used for a cookstove. It was set flat on the ground, for its legs were gone.

Back in the main room again Ruth looked more

closely at the mirror. It was very old. Some of the silver was gone from the back of the glass, but it had possibilities of beauty. She had been needing a mirror and these people certainly needed money. She asked them if they would sell it to her.

"Oh, no, mam, we couldn't do that. Our gran'-pappy brought that there with him when he come over the mountains in an oxcart. We couldn't rightly let it go."

This mirror episode was significant. There are many lovely old pieces of furniture tucked away in these hills, pieces brought across the mountains years ago. Antique collectors have not touched this field. They will find it a hard one to exploit, not because the owners appreciate the beauty or the extrinsic value of what they possess, but because "great-gran'pappy brought it with him from Virginny," and they wouldn't want to let it go.

These people could have bought a new mirror for much less than they might have received for the old one that needed resilvering. But it was not a mirror to them. It was *the* mirror, which could never be replaced. It was their title to respectability, their mark of claim to ancestors of substance and refinement, the bit of treasured beauty around which the continuity of their family dignity had been twined.

On their way home, Minnie and Ruth stopped for a few minutes at the one-room house of the Harpers. They were a young couple, recently married, so one room was enough. Jessie proudly showed their tiny home, bright with her own handwork and with gaily flowered oilcloth draperies and table cover. Would there be money enough to replace the oilcloth when this was peeled off? These young people were too happy and too thrilled with the pride of possession to wonder.

With the help of a government loan they had planted potatoes, only to lose them in the drouth. But it will take more than one season's failure to break their spirits. Five or six or ten years, with an equal number of dragging babies, will probably do it. It has happened to many others.

Hopeful planning for their own betterment is evident mainly among the young people. And they often show remarkable ingenuity in managing on nearly nothing. But it is difficult to keep struggling indefinitely against odds that seem insurmountable with only the aid of the meager resources at hand.

It is often possible to guess the age of a couple by looking at their house. A new home, like the Richardsons', may give incentive for a new start, but ordinarily a home which is tidy and attractive, with some semblance of curtains, with embroidered scarves and bedspreads, with plants on the porch, and with a neatly fenced yard brightened by flower beds, is the home of a young couple.

As they get older and the family grows, they have less time for frills. The bedspreads wear out and are replaced by more serviceable quilts. The curtains wear out and are not replaced. The children and the chickens ruin the flowers, so what use is there in planting more?

By the time the young family is grown the old folks have become accustomed to things as they are and seem to forget that they once had ideas of making them different; that they once declared that they would never let their place get to looking like the places of older people they had known. Their neighbors all know them as they are now, and there is not much use fixing things up. They have settled into a rut, and the easiest thing to do is to stay there. They are too tired to have much ambition left. They hope to "jest git by" till they die.

Ruth did not have an opportunity to visit the Ramseys' "real nice" house. They own many acres of level bottom land along the White River.

The river is especially beautiful there on crisp, cold mornings. Little swirls of mist rise above the whole surface, fleecy and white in the sunlight, making the water look just ready to boil. The river seems harmless, but a glance at a sharecropper's house in a flat field near by belies its innocent appearance. The house, much like a hillside cabin, is set high on stilts to raise it above any but a serious overflow, in order that the family need evacuate only in emergencies. A flatboat rests on the ground underneath, tied to one of the supporting posts, to be at hand in case of need. Between floods this boat serves as a chicken roost.

The Ramseys' house is approached by a drive spread with gravel from the bayou which joins the river not far away. This house, not of logs but of clapboards still showing the remains of a coat of white paint, is set on a rise of ground above the river's high-water level, with lower flat land all around it.

The house would be a very modest one in many parts of the country but in this section it seems

pretentious. It is "T"-shaped. The stem of the
"T," jutting out toward the road, is the sitting
room. This room has windows on three sides and is
flanked by porches. One of these porches is screened.
The thick cross of the "T" is divided into two bedrooms, a dining room, and a kitchen. There is no
running water in the house, but a pump comes up
through the floor of the porch off the kitchen.

The wooden walls are double, ceiled by a layer of
wide, smooth boards nailed to the studs and joists.
On these boards a light canvas is tacked, and real
wallpaper is pasted to the canvas. The wallpaper
has wrinkled and split as the boards beneath have
dried, but it is fresh and clean.

The upper sashes of the windows are nailed fast,
but the lower sashes may be raised and held up by
sticks, which stand on the window sills, leaning
against the frames, when not in use. The windows
are glazed, though some of the panes are cracked
and mended with strips of paper. Screen cloth
without a frame has been nailed over the lower
sash openings on the outside. There are shades and
flowered lace curtains hanging straight at the
windows.

The sitting-room floor is covered with a linoleum
rug. Here there is a set of overstuffed furniture
and two wicker rockers. There is an upright piano
and a battery radio set. A heating stove, set on a
decorated stove board, occupies a large space on one
side of the room. Between the stove and the wall,
logs are piled up for fuel. Brightly colored framed
prints adorn the walls. The piano top, the radio,
and every other available flat surface is loaded

A split-rail fence

Homemade gate latch

A finer house

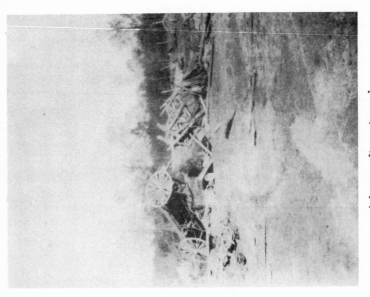

A house after a tornado

down with photographs and snapshots of relatives and friends.

The bedrooms have metal beds with thick feather pillows in embroidered slips, and unbleached muslin bedspreads decorated with appliqué. There are dressers and straight chairs also, and hooks for the clothes, which are partly concealed by a cretonne curtain hanging from a wire across the corner of the room, for here, too, there are no closets.

The dining room is furnished in golden oak. In the middle stands a round table with a heavy central pedestal. On the table top is a large hand-embroidered centerpiece and a china bowl of artificial fruit. There are leather-seated chairs, and a sideboard with beveled mirror. This sideboard is decked with bric-a-brac and cut glass.

In the kitchen is a kitchen cabinet and a wood range for cold-weather cooking, and for cooking the main meal all the year round. There is also a small oilstove for warm-weather supper preparation. The kitchen table is covered with bright patterned oilcloth.

There are pots and pans and tumblers and dishes and plated silverware—and mercerized tablecloths and napkins for use in the dining room. There is a shelf holding several oil lamps.

Behind the house there is a fine flock of white chickens. They are in a fenced yard with a chicken house at the far end. There is a smokehouse out there, too, and a storm cellar, a toilet with four sides and a roof, and a barn large enough to shelter the cows and mules and to hold many bales of hay in the loft. There is a small rail-fenced enclosure

for a sow and her litter, out of which they frequently root their way. Under a shed stands a small car,
almost new, with a license for the current year—
and the year is young yet. At the front of the yard,
on the roadway, is a one-room general store which
is opened by someone from the house when a cus-
tomer comes. Because this plantation is very large
it also has its own church and school. The Ramseys' home is indeed a "sight better'n most" houses
in the mountains.

The Martins are happy in their house because it
has been home for generations of them. The feet
of many loved ones have worn down the middle of
the doorstep. They remember the particular jolt
of the storm that took out some bit of chinking from
between the logs. They remember the frolic that
was responsible for the broken window, and the
day Grandpa found the keg and set it up as a step.
As children, they played house in the "dog trot"
and hide-and-seek in the loft. The hearth cracked
and sank before they were born. The same furniture has stood in the same place as long as they can
remember, and the same bucket has been used at
the well. They wouldn't want to give up dear familiar things and ways for the convenience of the
Richardsons' "newfangled" house.

The Richardsons are happy in their house. The
old familiar things are gone, so they can appreciate the convenience of a house without a passage,
the comparative ease of cleaning new floors, the
tightness of new walls covered with fresh blue
paper. They enjoy the prestige of owning the newest and finest house in the neighborhood. They

wouldn't want the Martins' old-fashioned house and they are sorry for the Cosseys.

The Cosseys are not content with their cabin, for there are many better ones around them. They would like another room and a wooden floor—but not quite enough to do anything about it. They are accustomed to their mode of living.

None of them envy the Ramseys. The Ramseys' house is outside of the circle of their experience. Even the sharecroppers on the place do not aspire to anything so fine.

Like the Richardsons, the Ramseys are content, because their house is among the best of those with which they are familiar.

But anyone from "outside," used to the conveniences of a modern house, would find it difficult to make himself comfortable in any mountain home.

4

Agriculture

My father left me three acres of land,
  Sing ivy, sing ivy;
My father left me three acres of land,
  Sing holly, go whistle and ivy!

ARISTOCRACY, IN THE HILLS, IS LARGELY DETER-
mined by the number of generations of a family
which have lived in the neighborhood, and by the
ownership of land. It is the ideal of every mountaineer to own his farm. Most hill families own,
or are at some stage in the process of acquiring or
losing, their forty or eighty acres.

A mountain baby is not born with a silver spoon
in his mouth. The farms are too small to be divided
among many sons. If a boy is not to inherit the
home place, his father will try to help him with the
purchase of tools and a team and to give him a cow
and some pigs, so that he can start out on land he
is purchasing or renting or homesteading for
himself.

Uncleared land is cheap in the hills. Forty acres
of good woodland can be bought for eighty dollars.
Cleared land is more expensive, so a man with little
capital, or one buying entirely on credit, will probably buy woodland. Most sections available for
homesteading are uncleared.

The first object of the new owner of the woodland is to clear enough of it to plant his crop. This may mean not only cutting down the trees and disposing of the wood, but also removing the stumps. Sometimes the farmer will put fire in the stumps and burn them out. The blaze and glow makes a weird fairyland of the hills at night. Or he may use small charges of dynamite to loosen the roots so that he can remove them. Or he may just plow around them and leave them to rot.

The trees in a field may be killed by collaring, and left standing for a long time. To collar a tree is to remove a strip of bark eight or ten inches wide all around the trunk, several feet above the ground. Cotton and corn do not flourish under leafy trees but dead trees take no nourishment from the soil and throw so little shadow that crops can be planted in among them.

Some owners have practically stripped their land of trees, but because clearing is such hard, slow work when done by primitive methods, the average man succeeds in freeing only that portion of his holdings which he expects actually to cultivate. This is done with no thought of forest preservation and no knowledge of the drainage problems involved. The most level section, or that most convenient to the house or to a road, is cleared.

Any value accruing to him from the trees on his property the farmer considers as incidental and temporary. They are primarily a handicap to his farming, and must be got out of the way. Trees that are large enough are sold for lumber or ties or staves. Some are used to build his house and sheds and some to make rail fences. The smaller wood he uses or sells for firewood or kindling.

After a hill field is cleared of trees it is still a rock field. Much of the land is strewn with gray rocks, averaging six inches in length and three in width. When one of them is freshly broken it is a rusty red inside. As this newly exposed surface is weathered it turns gray. Locally these are called "cotton rocks."

The Indians have a legend to account for the abundance of stones. At one time, they say, the mountains were smooth. The bushes and trees on them grew tall and straight and were spaced out so that both buffaloes and men could run easily, without needing to make paths. But the Indians, who had been friends of the buffaloes, learned to kill them. Then, to punish the men for their betrayal of friendship, the trees and bushes entangled themselves so that man must clear a way for himself, and the mountains, which were of solid stone, broke themselves into small pieces which would hurt man's feet when he ran over them.

Today man gathers the rocks by hand and piles them up to make fences to border his field, or dumps them on other land not yet cleared. After this the surface may look well until a heavy downpour washes the topsoil from the hill, exposing another layer of rocks. These are added to the fences, or again dumped elsewhere, until the farmer gets discouraged. Then he may let them alone and try to raise a crop through them. Or he may move to another farm.

In the Missouri Ozarks, when an outsider ex-

Uncleared land is cheap

Rocks piled up to make fences

Rich bottom land

presses wonder that anything will grow in such rocky soil, he may be told that when the land is plowed the rocks are turned under. Seed is then planted in the dirt which has been turned up. When a rain comes the dirt and seed are washed down and the rocks are on top once more, to hold in the moisture.

At best this hill land is poor. The soil is thin. A stranger to the Ozarks is not likely to succeed in farming here unless he has had special agricultural training. Experience in another part of the country will be of little use to him.

Much of the cleared land is intricately cut by gullies, and the rich topsoil is washed completely off some hills. The fields are small and uneven, sometimes tipped at an angle of forty-five degrees. The use of modern farm machinery is impossible on many of these farms. Such equipment is seldom found in the hills. What little is there is often left in the open, without any sort of shelter.

The little creeks may be great land destroyers. Ordinarily they tumble down from the higher hills, wander sedately across lower lands, and flow finally into the White or the Black or the Arkansas River. But when heavy rains send water tearing down the steep slopes into them, bringing topsoil, sand, and gravel from the fields, they rise suddenly. The water will race through the rocky ravines which the creek has cut, and when it reaches the flatter lands below, it will overflow the banks and spread over the fields, depositing gravel and sand there.

If the creek would return to its original course

when the water subsides, the same land would be inundated each time. But often, during the overflow, it has carved for itself another way, so the next time there is a heavy rain another part of the field will be covered. Thus, in time, a farmer's most level land may be all overspread with this undesirable wash which makes it useless—by the same water that carried the topsoil from his hill fields.

Being lighter than the sand and gravel, the good soil is carried farther. Having passed the leveler places, the supercharged little streams rush on again with this richer burden down to the river, and it, in turn, is overfilled. In some places the surging river roars through the stubborn rock defiles in its course, cutting them ever deeper. In others, released, it spreads itself out over the broad valleys which have not resisted it, covering them even to the hills, which have moved back long ago to let it pass. Here it shows its gratitude by depositing the rich soil which it has brought down from the mountainsides.

These flat, compliant river paths are "the bottoms"—so called in spite of being in the mountains. This bottom land, which may extend a mile or two back from the river's normal course, is rich and valuable. Some of these bottoms have long been noted as among the most fertile farming sections in America.

But the river is fickle. It may bring its gift of soil in the late winter and then, after all the crops are planted, it may come up again and wash them all away. Sometimes a farmer must plant his crop three times before the river lets it stay, and then it may be too late to ripen before the frost. In other years the river may never leave its banks, and then there will be bumper crops—unless the boll weevil is bad that season, or unless there is too little rainfall and the fields burn brown before they bear —thirsty fields baked under the sun within sight of the river.

While in the hills most men own, or hope to own, their land, in the bottoms a totally different system of landholding prevails. This fertile land being very desirable, a few families have gradually acquired most of it in large private holdings. Some inherited it from ancestors who came into the hills early and succeeded in upholding their claim to large sections. Others have won a share for themselves.

If a man has acquired more acres of land than his neighbors because of his superior industry and ability, without forgetting those whom he has outstripped, or if he has inherited what he owns and has used it well, he is loved and respected by his associates. But if he has gained what he possesses by imposing upon those about him, or if he has been too quick to foreclose on a mortgage, or if he has been unfair in collecting his crop rent, he is disliked and feared. While he will have no trouble in getting tenants—because dependent families are more plentiful than landlords to "furnish" them— his families will change frequently and they will take no interest in caring for his property. "You don't have to worry about him. He's able to take keer of hisself."

The plantation owners are comparatively rich men in their communities, but, considered by general standards, many of them are far from wealthy. Their children may go into town to high school, or, very infrequently, to college. Most of these men are not highly educated, and have no formal agricultural training whatever. Often their knowledge of farming is little superior to that of their poorer neighbors.

A large landowner may live on his own place, or he may live in town and have a hired overseer to live on his land while he himself goes out only occasionally to look after his interests.

In contrast to the custom of the hill farmer, the owners of bottom lands do not do the farming themselves. They divide their holdings into sections of ten, or fifteen, or perhaps as much as twenty-five acres, and let these out to many families. Each of these families has its own cotton patch and its corn patch and its garden patch.

If an Ozark plantation in the smooth bottom lands were cultivated as a unit, modern farm equipment could be used to advantage, as it is on plantations in the foothills and out of the mountains. It is impracticable to use it under the present system, however, with the land divided into small farms, and with these subdivided into smaller crop patches. So the plowing is done with a simple walking plow pulled by one or two mules, much of the planting is done by hand, the weeding and thinning ("chopping") are done with a hoe, and the picking is done by hand.

The more prosperous tenants on the land are the

"renters." A renter is independent of the planter in his daily life and to some extent in the use to which he puts the land. He owns his own team and tools, supplies his own seed, and clothes and feeds his own family. Only the land and the buildings he occupies are the property of the planter, and for their use he pays one fourth of the cotton and one third of the corn he raises.

The amount to be paid is always proportionate to the amount which is raised.

Cash rent is almost unheard of. The renter prefers the crop-rent system because it safeguards him if the yield is small. If crops are poor he and his landlord both lose. The landowner prefers the crop rent, with its possibility of liberal returns if the yield is large. He knows that in a bad year, when his crop rent is meager, he would probably be unable to collect cash rent from an equally hard-hit renter anyway. He would get only the satisfaction of putting him off his place for nonpayment. So they take their chances together.

If a man is lazy and cultivates less than his landlord thinks might have been possible, the renter finds himself looking for another place for the next season, while a more energetic family moves in where he has been. Or if his family is small, or there has been frequent illness, he may lose out in favor of a larger or healthier group, for the landlord wants as much as he can get from that piece of land.

The less prosperous man, who has nothing to offer but his labor and that of his household, becomes a "sharecropper." To him is assigned a portion of land with the accompanying buildings. His family is supplied with groceries and clothing from the planter's smokehouse and barn and store. Of these provisions a careful account is kept. At planting time the owner supplies him with seed and farm implements and a team. He has his own garden, planted with seed which his landlord has furnished, but during the summer the necessities which his garden does not provide still come to him from the plantation store.

When his crop is harvested he turns over to his landlord half of the cotton and half of the corn which he has raised, as payment of rent for the land and buildings and farming supplies, and in addition, from his own half, he reimburses him for the food and clothing he has received. This often leaves him with little or no surplus.

A limited number of families—those living nearest the "big house"—may have the opportunity during the winter to pay for what supplies they get by working on the planter's road, keeping up fences, milking, caring for the stock, butchering, and doing various odd jobs for which there is no regular employee. Some woman on the place will do the laundry for the "big house."

In recent years many large landholders have had their own credit curtailed and their incomes cut until they have been unable to provide supplies for their tenants during the lean months when they were getting no work in return.

One of Mr. Ramsey's tenants explains: "We ben sharecroppin' fer him a long time, and he's allers furnished us till this year. But now he ain't able to leave us have more'n a mite of meat and lard or a few molasses when I fix his fence, or somethin' a-ruther. Some of my work he cain't pay me fer noways till fall. He'll leave me keep some out of his share then. He ain't even able to furnish us no store account now, so we kinda ben up agin it."

This man lives in a tumbledown shack, a typical plantation tenant's house.

"The wind shore whistles through Mr. Ramsey's rent houses," he complains. "Such a sight of dobbin' has fell out from between the logs that they're plumb airish."

But he and his family like Mr. Ramsey. If they did not they would not have sharecropped for him for so many years. They are living as families have lived for years in these same cabins. Any possibility of changed methods or conditions has probably never occurred to them. *They* never expect to be landowners.

The present paternalistic system has the prestige of long usage. It can be traced back to slave days when, in the same way, the slaveholder was all things to those who belonged to him. True, the present white workers get some share of their labor for themselves, they are free to leave if they can find someplace else to go, and they work their own allotments of land. But in effect the former system still prevails, with the community of workers in their little cabins centered around and dependent upon the owner. He dictates the use of land, supplies the needs of his families, collects his rent, and to a great extent regulates the lives of his dependents.

Sharecroppers as a class are not overly energetic. The incentive is not great. The benefits are too remote. While the present system prevails, most of them will continue to be sharecroppers because they work best under the direction of another. They lack the initiative and managerial ability to succeed independently against the odds which face them.

But the fact that a man is a sharecropper at present does not indicate that he is of that type. He may have fallen to that state recently. Or he may have been just starting out as a young sharecropper at the onset of the depression. Because of that national catastrophe he may have had even less opportunity than he would ordinarily have had to improve his condition.

If his father is unable to help him to obtain a farm of his own, a young man has little choice but to become a day laborer or a sharecropper. If he is industrious, intelligent, trustworthy, and ambitious, he may gradually get ahead, eventually buying his own cow and raising his own pigs and chickens so that in succeeding years he will have milk and meat without having to go into debt for them.

Occasionally a sharecropper may be able slowly to accumulate enough to buy a team and tools of his own, and to arrange to supply his other needs on credit during the winter. Then he will become a renter instead of a sharecropper, retaining a larger proportion of his crop when it is harvested and enjoying greater liberty. In time he may be able to "crop out" (sublet) part of his rented land to

Farm Security Administration photograph by Shahn Starting out for a better land

Breaking ground

Cotton in the boll

Cotton held for a higher price

another family, or even to furnish them as sharecroppers. A true aristocrat may eventually become
independent.

In the last few years, however, the shift has more
often been in the other direction. Farmers have lost
the team and tools they owned.

There are not many tools to lose. Each family
would like to have a wagon, plows (perhaps a
breaking plow, a cultivator, and a harrow), and a
hoe for each member able to handle one, but many
do not have this much.

The loss of the team, to a store, a bank, or a
neighbor, or by death, is a terrible calamity in this
country. Over and over again one hears the cry,
"We shore have ben hard hit. We lost a mule and
a mare this winter." Or, "We had one mule and it
died, and we bought another'n on credit and they
taken it back 'cause we couldn't pay." Or, "We had
a mule lay down and die yesterday. We didn't even
know there was nothin' wrong, but when it didn't
come in last evenin', Enness went out to hunt it
and found it stiff and cold in the woodlot. It warn't
much of a critter, jest a frame of a mule, I reckon,
but we thought we could work it with our other'n,
come spring, and Enness had a chance to git it fer
ten dollars, to be paid in wood. The wood hain't all
ben tuck over yit. Now the other nag'll have to haul
it all by its own self."

It is hard to make a crop without a team. Without at least one mule a man may be forced to become a sharecropper. A mule is relatively expensive. When one dies it is ordinarily one of two, or
perhaps the only one, the farmer owns. And when

it is gone, it's gone, with nothing left to show for the sacrifice that bought it.

If a man can get a mule in the spring on credit he can manage to plant, even though he lose the animal again in the fall. But when times are hard it becomes increasingly difficult to find an owner who is willing to make a credit transaction, knowing that such a sale is likely not to amount to permanent disposal.

At present the number of persons unable to "supply theirselves" is so great that there are not enough share-crop places to go around. A man may be left out if his reputation for having an industrious family is questionable, or if he is put off the farm where he has been living so late in the season that all the other places have been promised to earlier applicants.

Then he and his family have no choice but to become day laborers, picking up jobs where they can, and "livin' slim" when the jobs are scarce. During cotton chopping and picking seasons there may be work for extra hands on farms where a man has planted more than his own family can properly care for. Then the day laborer may earn fifty or sixty or seventy-five cents a day. In good times and when laborers are few, some farmers used to pay a man even as much as one dollar a day.

He may receive this amount in cash, or it may be paid in foodstuffs. And so he goes through another year, hoping to beat someone else to a share crop next season.

Some, on account of bad reputation or indolence, never succeed in finding a place, and they become regular crop followers. Others become crop followers because they prefer the freedom and like to get a little cash to jingle in their pockets.

These seasonal movers, while considering the mountains their home, will go fifty miles south in the early spring to pick berries in the great strawberry plantations. While there, they live in tents or shacks belonging to the owners of the berry fields. They are paid very little for the work, but it is "cash money."

Carnivals arrange to be near the berry fields during picking season.

When the berries are gone, these families will return to the fertile river-bottom land again to chop the corn and cotton. Then in the fall they will travel north into the panhandle bottom land of Missouri and pick cotton until nearly Christmastime. When the cotton is all picked they will come home again with money in their pockets and stay until time to start their circuit again early the next May. This schedule and this mode of living proved satisfactory to a good many so long as there was enough cotton for everyone to pick, but now they may not always find work.

In the last few years some of the more aggressive men, particularly the younger men who are comparatively footloose and are unwilling to sit idle and wait for better times, have left home to look not for seasonal but for regular work elsewhere. When a man can find no land on which to put a crop, and when there are many more laborers than jobs, there is not much choice but to accept relief if he stays at home, and there seems to be nothing to lose by going elsewhere. No place could be worse than the place where he is, he reasons, and some other place might be better. It will be preferable to spend his time investigating the possibilities, even though he be disappointed, than to do nothing.

It must be very discouraging as he goes hopefully toward that other place, to meet someone from there journeying just as hopefully toward the place which he himself has just left.

If a man has a small family and any sort of a car that will still go, he may load them in and start out for that better land that is just over the next hill—and the next.

But if the aggressive man has a large family, or if he must depend upon generous, foolhardy motorists for his transportation, then he goes alone.

For a long time his wife may not know where her husband is. She may only know that he left to look for work. If he cannot write—and if his family cannot read, even though he send a letter— there is not much chance of keeping them informed as to his whereabouts and circumstances. If his stay is protracted and the family has no idea when to expect him home, they may be asked to leave the house which they are occupying, or they may go to live with relatives for company or for help. If they move far, the husband may have a lengthy search before finding them when he at last returns.

But few men in the hills have enough initiative or imagination to induce them to leave. The familiar things seem safer; hence, most of them stay at home and wish for better times.

The mountaineer, however, unless he owns, and can keep, his land, is accustomed to moving often within a limited radius. Some other farm appeals more to him—or some other farmer looks better to his landlord. Hill families move to the bottoms to find better land. Families move from the bottoms to the hills to get away from the danger of overflows, or in disgust at the loss caused thereby.

If a man has no way of moving his goods, he may find it necessary to give away his cow or the chickens in exchange for the use of a wagon and team. So the poorer family often arrives at the new location with no stock.

There is little money in circulation in the hills. Barter is the chief medium of exchange. A man who is unable to find a place to put in a share crop may arrange to "work through the crop" of another man in exchange for "six acres of cotton, a watermelon patch, and a corn patch," or some other apportionment. His friend may even agree to furnish him credit and supplies while the crops are growing and be repaid from the six acres of cotton.

This arrangement differs from the share-crop system in that in this case he and his family work in the fields someone else is cultivating, and in the other they cultivate a certain section by themselves. This is not a general and recognized procedure, but just an arrangement between friends.

A woman may do a family washing for someone who is ill, in exchange for meat or lard or molasses. She may milk another's cows in exchange for some of the milk, or feed the chickens for eggs.

A man may plow a neighbor's field and in return

be allowed to use his neighbor's horses to plow his own field. He may be paid with peas or beans or feed for cutting his neighbor's wood, or with meat for butchering.

The wife sends eggs or chickens or cream to town to trade for groceries or even for drygoods. The barter system has limited possibilities for trading in town, for the stores are quickly supplied each Saturday with all the eggs and hens and cream they can use. So, even though his material for barter may not be exhausted, a man's family may want for the things which require cash, unless he has a cash balance from his year's crop.

The farmer who has raised more feed than he needs—more corn or cottonseed or hay—will use this surplus to pay for help on his farm or will trade some of it with one who has an excess of things that he lacks—potatoes, perhaps, or beans, or pigs, or chickens. But when his surplus is gone and he has nothing more to trade, his medium of exchange is gone, and he in turn must find someone who still has the things he needs and is willing to allow him to acquire them by working for them. When his neighbors have disposed of their over-supply his possibility of meeting his own needs is blocked, unless he is fortunate enough to find a man who has money which he is willing to exchange for labor. Such men are scarce and hard to find.

"Tom's ben out cuttin' wood fer nigh onto a week. He gits paid in first one junk and then another, but we ben gittin' enough to scrape along. He fetched home a hog and some taters fer some wood, and old lady Thomas give him some corn fer helpin' butcher. But he don't git no cash money."

Gradually, as the families in a community exchange what they can spare for what they lack, the balance is reached and barter is at a standstill. Sometimes this does not happen in the course of a year. In years when there has been drouth or flood to curtail the crops, this balance is reached early, and want and even starvation may result.

Poor and rocky soil is not the only factor behind the dire poverty of the hills people. Farming methods and the use to which the land is put are also largely responsible.

Most of the mountaineers have been farmers all their lives, so they have as much agricultural knowledge as has been available to them, but that is scant. The way that pappy farmed is good enough—or the only way that son knows. His farm practices are based more on superstition than science.

His farming equipment is outmoded or inferior or insufficient.

If he has no team he may put in what crop he can with a hoe, or "fork it in." From the kitchen garden he digs potatoes enough for a meal with an ordinary four-tined kitchen fork. He explains his use of this tool by saying that if the potatoes are not large enough to eat they may be pressed back into the earth and will grow again after this gentle exploration, whereas they will grow no more if they have been rudely disturbed with a garden fork.

The Ozark farmer does not want suggestions for bettering his methods.

A stranger taking up land in the hills and introducing methods of his own will probably be ridiculed. When the poor spot he has treated with a little fertilizer begins to bear like the surrounding land, his mocking neighbor may surreptitiously experiment with a little of the same treatment for that spot on his own land which he had long ago abandoned as worthless.

But teaching is not so well accepted. In the last few years there have been county agents who advocate terracing. They recommend a change from cotton to some other crop. They urge rotation of crops and enrichment of soil. Many fields have been used for the same crop year after year until the soil is quite worn out.

But much of their "preachment" falls on deaf ears, if it reaches them at all, for "didn't Pappy raise cotton here? And didn't his pappy what come here from Georgy? These young smart alecks what never cropped in these hills in their lives can't tell us none of their newfangled idears. We ben farmin' here all our lives, and we know!"

Because of the early frosts and the relatively thin soil in the Ozark highlands, cotton farming there does not pay. And yet cotton is the principal crop of this section.

It is said to be suitable for orchards, for vineyards, or for the raising of sheep or goats. But the people who till the soil know little of the advantages, and less of the care, of such things. And they have no margin on which to live while they experiment, even if they were convinced that such a shift would be wise. Co-operative dairying may someday be a profitable hill industry. It is already being developed in the foothills. Before it can become so in the hinterland, however, mountaineers will need to learn to work together, and more good roads will have to be built to facilitate milk and cream collection.

The University of Arkansas has recently established a Livestock and Forestry Experiment Station in the Ozarks. Various pasture grasses and clovers, forage, feed and truck crops, cotton and fruits are being tested to determine their adaptability to typical Ozark soil and topography. The suitability of this region for various sorts of livestock and trees is also being tried. These experiments, as knowledge of them gradually filters through the hills, should eventually result in more profitable use of the land.

Meanwhile the cotton still goes in year after year. And if there is no overflow and the rain falls at the right time and in sufficient quantities and the frost doesn't come too soon, the family makes enough money to pay its bills and may have enough left to carry it through the winter.

Another principal cause of hunger in the hills is the failure of most farmers to raise feed crops to care for the needs of the family and the stock. A very few may plant enough corn to supply feed for the stock, meal for the family, and seed for the next year. A few may plant some other feed crop and enough vegetables to last until the next crop is ready. But in many cases even this minimum for home consumption is not raised. Most families use every bit of the land they plant, except the meager kitchen garden space, for cash crops, hoping to sell them for enough to pay their debts and buy much of their winter food and feed from town. As a result, if the cash crop fails, they have neither cash nor food nor feed, and their debt must grow rather than diminish.

The stock is fed when there is feed, and the rest of the time the animals have to wander freely and "fend fer theirselves." But hogs that have run wild in the woods don't fatten enough to make good meat or lard. And cows not properly fed will not give milk, nor chickens eggs, and mules can't work if they are nearly starved. So when feed is scarce, the unfortunate results are many.

A refrain that becomes familiar because of continued repetition is, "We got a cow but she ain't a-givin' no milk." "Shore, we got a few hens but they ain't a-layin' none." "Yes siree! We butchered, but the hogs was so porely we didn't git no lard."

A few families in the hills have been granted rural rehabilitation loans by the Federal Government. Widely scattered farms are selected for these loans in order that many may have an opportunity to observe the results. Under this plan a farmer has been allowed to plant only food and feed crops at first, and the various parts of his crop have been put on the sections of his land best suited to them, as determined by an expert agriculturalist. Later on he is allowed to raise some "cash crops" in addition to sufficient food and feed. But at first he has had to concentrate on doing the thing that he and his neighbors have so long failed to do, that is, raise enough food and feed to supply both his family and his stock through the whole year. If the mountaineers could learn to do that first, and then use what land and time remain for the cash crop, there would be much less hunger among them. But so far this training has affected very few.

A few more have been encouraged to seed pastures and grow legumes to enrich the soil in order to qualify for benefit payments under the Soil Conservation program.

In the rich bottom lands along the river, corn grows well. It is raised here in abundance as a cash crop, and though it may be washed out time and again and need to be replanted, its yield in a good crop year is large enough to pay for all the loss. But in both bottoms and hill sections cotton is the main cash crop.

How well does it pay? An acre of cotton in the bottoms will yield about 175 pounds. A bale of cotton weighs about 500 pounds. When cotton is selling at ten cents a pound, a bale will be worth about $50. On nine or ten acres, a farmer will raise about three bales, with a cash value of $150.

If he owns his farm, he will have the whole $150 to use to pay his taxes and to feed and clothe his family. If he is a renter, one fourth of his cotton will go to the landowner and he will have $112.50 to care for his family and stock. If he is a sharecropper, one half will go to the owner and he will have $75 left with which to get ahead.

If all goes well and he has plenty of corn and a good garden, if the little chicks live and he gets enough eggs to trade for his small grocery needs, if he has feed enough to keep his chickens laying and to fatten the hogs for meat, and if his sorghum patch is good, he will be able to manage—unless he owes too much.

The man in the bottoms will probably have the use of a team instead of a single mule, and so he could care for a larger acreage. But nine or ten acres may be the limit of his allotment of cotton land by the owner. Other families need the other land.

In the hills more men own their farms. But cotton does not grow so well. A much larger acreage must be planted to furnish the same yield, and the planting and care is much more difficult. Thus, even though a farmer owns a team so that he can scratch through the rocks on twelve or fifteen acres, he will have no more cotton to show for his labor than the bottoms farmer gets from his ten acres. And if he has but one mule, planting six acres of cotton will be an accomplishment.

A hill farmer who owned his farm had a bad year, and hence no money to carry him through the winter and summer and up until late fall, when he could expect to sell his crop. So he went into town to the big general store. There he arranged for credit and got his year's supply of clothing for his family, and his coffee, sugar, flour, and other cash items.

He got some harness that was essential if he were to use his team (which he had bought on credit), and a roll of fence wire, and gave a mortgage on his farm in exchange for all this.

His corn crop having failed, he ran out of feed for his stock in January, so he went back into town for more. Because he used this primarily for his team, his hogs did not fatten well, and soon he was out of meat and lard.

There were doctor bills. In February there was an epidemic of scarlet fever and all the children were sick. One little boy died. In the spring there was a new baby.

When it was time for spring planting he fortunately had enough cottonseed left after using much of it for feed, but he needed seed of other kinds, so he went back to town for it.

In the fall he loaded his cotton into his wagon and took it to the gin and then on into town. He received $150 from the cotton broker who bought it at the government price.

He found that his store bill was $156, including the interest which was charged him. On such fall credit transactions where a mortgage is required, the interest rate is usually 25 per cent or higher. This is not itemized as interest but is buried in the total. The purchaser does not know what things would have cost him if he had paid cash.

He paid his $150 on the bill and brought two of his hogs to town the next week to pay the balance. He had nothing left for the doctor, nor to pay his taxes. And he lost his team.

The man who had sold him the team and had to take it back, lost little. He had another team of his own, and the would-be purchaser had fed this one for him for a season.

When he brought the two hogs in to complete

payment on his old bill, he arranged for credit with
the store again, and took another winter's supplies
back home with him. In the spring he would buy
another team, or perhaps just one mule, on credit,
and hope to pay for it out of the next crop.

This is not an unusual case. There are so many
actual cases like it that it would not even excite
any interest locally. A large number of the mountaineers live on credit. They marry on nothing, and
raise a family and go on, year after year, running
always a year behind in their bills. Many families
owe more than they can possibly make from a
year's crop before it is even planted.

If a drouth hits the mountains, families that
have been living on credit one year behind are put
two years behind. And if there are two dry years
in succession, or if there is a flood, or if the bottom drops out of the cotton market, such families
cannot pay their bills and consequently lose their
teams, or cows, or even the farm tools and harness
which they have mortgaged. And if this happens
often, and credit is tight, and these families fail
to pay their taxes for two years in succession, they
lose their little plots of land. The farms are sold
at auction so that the state may collect the delin-
quent taxes out of the proceeds. If there are no
other bidders, the state buys the land. In that case
a man is sometimes able to redeem his farm from
the state if he can scrape together enough money
before the land has been disposed of in some other
way.

The stores are accustomed to this credit system.
The volume of their trade has been of this sort;

but they have seldom lost anything, for a man has got his supplies by mortgaging something valuable enough to cover the bill.

In the last few years, however, the stores have had to cut down on these transactions, both because their own credit has been curtailed and they are required to have a greater percentage of cash to pay their own bills, and because so many families have lost their valuable collateral.

The banks, too, have shut down on credit almost entirely. In Arkansas they may legally charge 6 to 10 per cent interest on loans, which are more difficult to secure than is store credit. To many farmers, the bank is known only as a lending institution. They may never in their lives have had enough cash together at one time to open an account, and they would perhaps not trust the bank with cash if they did have extra.

So, during the depression, families have got more behind, and there have been more families needing share crops, and the landowners have had less to furnish them with, and so it has gone from bad to worse.

As a condition which affects stocks and bonds and dividend checks the depression has not had great effect on these people, but as it has lowered the price paid them for what they have to sell and has curtailed credit, it has hurt. And they have had less to sell at any price because there has been a series of floods and drouths which have been disastrous to them. One of the worst floods in recent years came in 1927, almost the last season when they might have received high prices for their crops.

Even without drouth or flood or low prices, there has always been the possibility of sickness coming to create a crisis for the individual family, but it was easier to tide over such emergencies when debts were not so great, when credit was more easily available, and when friends and relatives had something to share. During the last few years, with debts constantly increasing, and with everyone else in the same predicament, the situation has been desperate for many.

Many families, which, under normal conditions, would have continued to be self-supporting and which will undoubtedly become independent again, had never been able to accumulate enough to be ready to meet such a series of disasters.

Some who had been "comfortably fixed" in years gone by have lost their savings suddenly. More had barely clung to the edge of independence all their lives, and the drop of prices and limiting of credit were all that was necessary to push them off into dependency. And how they have shrunk from it!

5

Other Occupations

Little ships must keep the shore;
Larger ships may venture more.

ASIDE FROM AGRICULTURE, POSSIBILITIES FOR EARN-
ing a living in the hills are decidedly limited.

There is almost no professional work. A very
few doctors have returned to their mountain homes
after completing their education, but lawyers and
other professional men must look to larger centers
of population for their clientele.

Occasionally there may be a little carpentry
work, a barn or a shed to be built, or a fence to be
run.

Ordinarily a family requires no outside help for
such undertakings, especially if the hiring of help
necessitates paying in cash. But a man may be
allowed to work out a debt in some such way.

Few public buildings—schools and churches—
are constructed, and the labor for the erection of
a church will often be donated.

The abundance of wood furnishes some work.
There is a limit to the market for firewood. Each
man in the hills has his own, and the town market
is quickly supplied. A man sells a rick of wood—
a pile eight feet long by four feet high, by sixteen
or twenty or twenty-four inches wide—for about

one dollar and twenty-five cents. It is no wonder that this is the principal heating and cooking fuel. If he cuts wood for another man he gets only fifty cents for his labor and the owner of the wood receives seventy-five cents.

There are sawmills which buy some larger timber, but a sawmill owner usually has his own woodland. When he wants some of this cleared he will put up tents and get several families to move into his woods. In addition to furnishing this shelter he may pay a man fifty cents a day while the job lasts. He will also have several men working for him in the mill, both to trim down his own logs and to make planks of the logs brought to him by others for planing. The mill hands may receive twenty-four cents an hour, but the employment is not steady.

There is a market for railroad ties. These are cut and hauled to some point along the railroad right of way for inspection. The scrutiny is very rigid. A man may cut ties for days and in the inspection have all but one or two of them declared culls. For the accepted ties he will get a few cents apiece, for the culls nothing.

Stave mills employ men for the cutting of barrel staves, when they receive orders from coopers. When the question of the repeal of the Eighteenth Amendment was pending, the promise was made that repeal would put many men to work in the local mills. Just before the polling time the stave market boomed. A good many men were taken from the relief rolls for jobs paying one dollar and fifty cents a day. But soon after the question of repeal was settled the orders stopped, and the recently employed men, who had piled the yards full of drying stave bolts, were back on the relief rolls.

A man with a truck may do nothing but wood hauling, at one dollar a day, if he can find enough jobs to keep himself busy and pay for the upkeep of his vehicle. He will probably have bought a secondhand truck on credit, and must earn enough to meet the payments. He will use it in the woods where there are no roads, so repairs will be necessary frequently. His license and gasoline will be expensive. As a result there are few trucks operated in the mountains, and the man who owns one is in constant fear of losing it, or having to discontinue its use without being able to sell it. Most of the wood is hauled in wagons for, as one mountaineer said, "Bein' in debt is like a fly in molasses, sweet a-gittin' in and hell a-gittin' out."

The Ozarks are famous for marble of many colors. The only black marble in the United States is found here. A man can make two dollars and a half a day and live in a company house, when the quarries are operating. But with the curtailment of building over the whole country the demand for marble has dwindled until the quarries have been worked hardly at all in several years.

There is limestone. The large lime kilns employed a good many men and housed their families in good times, but the number has been decreased there, too, in recent years.

The largest manganese beds in the country are in these hills. The mining system is this: a mining company owns miles of mountain land. On this they build houses which they turn over to families who are interested in mining. These families will plant gardens but will probably not care to take time to plant larger crops. They may dig into the mountains on the mine company's land, wherever they choose, trying to find manganese near the surface. If they succeed in finding it they load it into sacks and the company collects the sacks, examines the concentration of the dirt and pays them accordingly. If they are unsuccessful in finding the ore they get nothing. They keep looking, however, for there is always the chance that they may strike a productive "dig." The families do not become wealthy, nor much more than ward off starvation, but hope springs eternal.

There are great natural resources in the Ozarks but they have scarcely been touched, as yet, because of their inaccessability and because of lack of capital with which to develop them.

Local place names, such as Greasy Cove or Greasy Bend, might suggest a possibility of oil in this hill country. On some streams, when the water is quiet, a black oily film covers the surface. With the belief that there is oil, some drilling has been done, but none, so far, with success. Always the word has come, "It must be deeper," "A little deeper yet," and always the money has run out before the drilling has gone deep enough.

Perhaps the names are not significant. Oil Trough was not named because of petroleum in the locality but because of bears. At one time bears were numerous in that section of the Ozarks. Bear

Cutting slabs with a circular saw

Getting out timber

Houseboat in a flood

Good fishing

Stock auction sale day

oil was stored in troughs made of hollow logs and shipped to Memphis from this point on the White River.

Along the rivers men make a living, of a sort, by fishing and mussel-shell digging.

For fishing, "trotlines" (the original word was "trawl line") are strung across the river or a creek, weighted down so that they will not interfere with the passage of boats. These lines are of very heavy fishing cord with large hooks attached every two or three feet. The fisherman "runs" (examines) his lines twice a day to get what he has caught and to replace bait stolen by small fish. The streams abound in buffalo, drum, and catfish. Sometimes catfish weighing seventy-five or eighty pounds are caught on "trotlines."

In the White and Black Rivers there are quantities of mussels. Double scoops not unlike the mollusks for which they probe are used for shell gathering. The scoop, about a foot wide, is attached to the end of a long handle. The upper "jaw" is operated with an improvised lever on this handle.

Mussels are cooked in a pot over a fire on the riverbank in order to get the shells open. The flesh is used for fish bait.

The mussels are dug primarily for the value of the shells as button material. Then there is always the romantic possibility of finding a rare pearl. The quality of these Arkansas pearls is world famous.

Many of the fishermen live on the riverbank in houseboats. Most of the time the boats rest on the shore. In case of overflow they rise with the water.

One original man has built an ordinary log cabin at the river's edge. Instead of being set on the ground, it is built on a rectangular frame made of four choctaw logs, each about three feet in diameter, strapped together at the corners. Choctaw wood is porous and lighter than cork. This foundation is anchored, by slack cables, to near-by trees, so that in case of flood, the house will be floated, high and dry, but will not be washed away.

A very few families have started goat ranches but they have done so at the expense of their popularity with their neighbors. Friends cease to drop in to see the rancher's family because of the odor of the goats. And the members of the family may carry a trace of that odor about with them wherever they go. At least their farmer friends think so.

Goat raising does not appeal to many as worth this loss of friends. The mountaineers, and most of the townspeople, for that matter, have not learned to eat lamb or mutton, and goat raisers themselves declare that goat meat is "too porely fer 'em to eat." The demand for goat milk has not been developed to any great extent. At present the only profit likely to be realized from sheep or goats is from the wool and hair and skin.

Cotton gins scattered through the hills each employ two or three men during the ginning season. These employees cultivate their own crops in addition to doing their gin work. A farmer may run a gristmill or a blacksmith shop. All of these furnish temporary seasonal employments which do not interfere seriously with agricultural pursuits.

They simply augment the incomes of those already farming. The gins pay cash wages. These other part-time jobs are paid for by meal toll or molasses or hay or some other commodity.

In the woods there are pecan and black walnut trees in abundance. Some families supplement their incomes somewhat by gathering these nuts and selling them to the stores or directly to the housewives, or by selling the nut kernels which they have picked out on long winter days. At Christmastime boys peddle bunches of holly and mistletoe.

Another means of making at least part of a livelihood is by basket weaving, with splints and willows. It takes an experienced gatherer to find the reeds and white oak saplings at just the right stage at which, after proper soaking, the strips can be bent without breaking.

Some persons have adopted, as a winter occupation, the making of furniture from saplings. For this, too, the selection of wood at exactly the right stage is an art. They make settees, armchairs, rockers, fern stands, and flower baskets. The market is limited. They complain that anyone who can afford a living-room set wants something finer than they can make, and those who would be satisfied with rustic articles cannot afford to buy them. With the vogue for outdoor living this furniture is becoming increasingly popular for garden use, however, so the market is growing.

Another seasonal work which does not interfere with farming is hunting and trapping, both for meat and pelts. There are rabbits and opossum and skunk, and other wilder and less plentiful game.

Frogs are caught and sold for their legs. Most of them are shipped out of the hills to city markets. "Do you know how to ketch frogs?" a mountaineer asks. "You go out with a lantern at night. Them as has 'em uses a flashlight. You walk along a crick. The toad-frogs are a-settin' on the bank a-hollerin'. When you find one you shine your light in his eyes. Hit sorter paralyzes him, and you kin walk right up to him and pick him up. Fellers with cars hunt rabbits that-a-way. One feller sets on the hood with a gun. When the headlight shines in a rabbit's eyes he stops stock still so's the feller kin shoot him."

Another product of the hills is ginseng.

One farmer explained, "I heerd tell that they buy ginseng roots to make medicine out of. They grow around in these here woods some but they're mighty skeerce. I'm larnin' how to raise 'em and spread 'em. I've dug up all the roots I could find hereabouts and have planted 'em in a patch up yonder on the hill there. We had ought to make a good livin' on 'em once they grow enough fer me to sell off 'em, but that'll be a right smart while, fer they grow powerful slow. Hit takes nigh onto seven year fer a root to git old enough to sell, and the older they be, the better."

The roots weigh one-and-a-half to four ounces apiece when they are fresh and one-half to one-and-a-third ounces dry. Two acres, planted 100,000 roots to an acre, will produce 25,000 roots a year by multiplication. The wholesale price in New York

City is from twelve to thirteen dollars a pound. This mountaineer's patch was very small.

He probably did not know that little or no ginseng is used in the United States but that in China the roots are supposed to have extraordinary virtues as a remedy for almost all diseases, particularly for mental and physical exhaustion. Consequently, there is a profitable export market for American ginseng.

In his book, *My Country and My People*, Lin Yutang says of the Chinese, "It stands to reason that ... we should have stumbled upon important discoveries, as most scientific or medical discoveries have been stumbled upon. For one thing, we have discovered the magic qualities of ginseng, for which I am willing to give personal testimony as to its being the most enduring and most energy giving tonic known to mankind, distinguished by the slowness and gentleness of its action."

Lin Yutang, *My Country and My People*. New York: The John Day Company.

6

Ancestry

I lost my mare in Lincoln Lane,
And couldn't tell where to find her,
Till she came home both lame and blind,
With never a tail behind her.

THEORIES OF THE DERIVATION OF THE WORD "Ozark" tell something of the early inhabitants of this region. It has been suggested that it is a combination of the word "Osage," a name of French origin given to an Indian tribe which is said to have been living in the mountains when De Soto explored the country in 1541, and of "Arkansas." Another explanation is that it is a shortening of the French "Aux Arkansas" to "Aux Arcs," spelled phonetically. A third theory is based upon the fact that the Indians found the wood of the Osage orange tree especially suitable for making bows. The French called the tree "Bois d'arc" (bow wood) which became "Bodark." Many of these trees were found in the Ozark region, and there so many Indians went for their bow wood that French trappers spoke of their destination as "the bow mountains" or "Montagnes aux arcs." Gradually this was shortened to "Aux arcs."

The name "Arkansas" is also accounted for in various ways. Some say that it was first appropri-

ately used to described the river which still bears
the name. According to this explanation, it is the
Indian word "kansas" (smoky water) with the
French "arc" (bow or bend) prefixed.

Others say that it was the name of a superior
tribe of Indians, the Arkansa, and that it was
spelled in many ways by early French writers, for
example: Arkansea, Acanca, Akanssa, Accanes,
Alkansa, Arkensaw.

It may have been the name of a tribe of Indians
who separated from the Kansas Nation. These Indians were renowned for the fine bows they made
and came to be known as the "bow"—or "arc"—
Kansas Indians.

According to an Indian legend, Okanasa (bushy
head) was a great chief. The river on which his
tribe lived was named for him because a sketch of
the river and the many small streams which flowed
into it clearly resembled a "bushy head." As a
fulfillment of prophecy, after Okanasa had been
taken bodily from the presence of his people by the
hand of the Great Spirit, he shouted back to them
the new pronunciation of his name, which was
henceforth to be used in designating the tribe, the
river, and the land on both sides—Arkansaw.

Long before the Indians or the French came to
Arkansas the Ozarks were the home of the Rock
Shelter people. Archaeologists differ in their esti-
mates of the antiquity of these people. Some say
that they inhabited the mountains from 1,800 to
3,000 years ago. Others claim that they may have
lived there during the end of the ice age, about
20,000 years ago. There is no evidence that they

were in any way connected with the Indians which lived there later.

Many Indian tribes have lived in Arkansas. Some have sojourned long and the stay of others has been brief—an incident in their westward trek. There is record that the Chicasaws, Ozarks, Delawares, Cherokees, Caddoes, Pawnees, Tunicas, Quapaws, Osages, Choctaws, Arkansas, Shawnees, and perhaps others have lived there at some time in their history.

De la Vega, in recounting De Soto's experiences of 1541, speaks of the Cherokees as coming from their mountain homes to bathe in the hot pools of what is now Hot Springs. The old Cherokee Nation was in Tennessee and Georgia. In 1817 they surrendered that land to the United States Government in exchange for a large tract of northwestern Arkansas. They were moved on from there into Oklahoma by treaty, in 1828.

Similarly the other tribes also had gone West. The Osages had relinquished the last of their Arkansas territory in 1825. But Indians have left their names for streams and hills, trees, and settlements. There are towns today called Chickalah, Pocahontas, Osceola, Wabbaseka, and Powhatan (now pronounced Pow-hat'-an).

The first white men to see the Ozarks were Spaniards. It is possible that followers of Francisco de Coronado visited them in about 1540. The oldest definite records of the explorations of white men recount the experiences of Hernando de Soto and his men, in the territory now called Arkansas, in 1541. The Spaniards left the new world as sud-

The Ozarks are old, old mountains

White River bluffs

Their great-grandparents settled in the Ozarks

A new house in the old manner

denly as they had come, and the white man became
legendary to the Indians.

More than a hundred years had passed when, in
1673, strange white men again appeared. These
men were French, Jesuit missionaries, Jacques
Marquette and Louis Joliet.

In about 1682 came René Robert Cavaelier,
Sieur de La Salle, to claim all the country watered
by the Mississippi and its tributaries, for the King
of France. Some of his men, under the leadership
of Henri de Tonti, established Arkansas Post, the
first white settlement in Arkansas, in about 1686.
Their intention, according to De Tonti, "was only
to humanize and civilize the savages by associating
with them."

More Frenchmen came, but few stayed. The
French were not efficient colonizers. Their pioneering groups were small, their numbers were not
maintained by sufficient recruits from the homeland, and few of them came to establish homes in
the new world. They came to find wealth or ad-
venture or to Christianize the natives, and return.
By 1785 there were only 196 white persons in
Arkansas.

The Ozark region belonged alternately to the
French, the Spanish, and the French again. The
French have left their mark on names, as the Indians have. Many small streams are "bayous"
(dead streams) in these mountains. Many town
names bear the French suffix "ville." Some are
named for French explorers. Some names have
been so changed that their French origin is scarcely
discernible. "Salado" is the present name of a

creek. The French called it "Sel d'eau" (salt water). On old maps it is shown as "Sally Doe," "Salladoe," "Salidoe," and "Salladore."

As the eastern part of our country was settled, some hunters and traders found their way into the Ozarks. But they came only for profit and then returned to their homes east of the Mississippi.

The ancestors of the first permanent settlers had come from still farther east.

In 1607, James I of England drove the Hibernians out of six counties of Ulster in northern Ireland, and imported Scotch families to colonize this confiscated territory. These Scotch-Irish became dissatisfied with the economic and religious regulations and restrictions imposed on them by the British government, and when their leases in Ulster expired in about 1700, many of them immigrated to America. This flow of Scotch-Irish continued undiminished until the time of the American Revolution.

Those who came were aggressive and since, by habit and tradition they were a border people, they began to find their way to the Western frontier, then in Pennsylvania. On this extreme western fringe of settlement there were also Germans from the Palatinate (Pennsylvania-Dutch) and Irish. Together they served as buffers between the Indians to the west and the seaboard settlers to the east.

As the population grew these frontiersmen began to feel crowded and moved farther west into the Alleghanies. They might have continued over the mountains had not the country beyond the Susquehanna River been so rocky and poor that the land to the southwest and south, in Maryland and Virginia, seemed more promising. Therefore the overflow of settlers moved in those directions. Some went on to the lowlands of the south which were already occupied by English who had gone directly there. But many, to whom the highlands were more like their old homeland, preferred to stay in them, following the watercourses to their sources, then crossing a ridge and going farther still. In both highlands and lowlands the population was now predominantly Anglo-Saxon—sturdy, honest, and thrifty.

By 1768 the frontier had been pushed into North Carolina and Tennessee. The first or the most able comers claimed the rich land along the rivers. Others moved farther on or settled along the smaller streams. As families grew or neighbors got too close the more ambitious and venturesome and those who were unanchored, moved farther west. Daniel Boone went into Kentucky in 1769, and before long others were following him. By 1800 the vanguard had reached Arkansas.

In 1803, when the United States purchased the Louisiana Territory, which included the Ozark region, there were only 368 non-Indians in Arkansas. Some of these were hunters and traders and others were settlers.

After this purchase the influx of settlers from the East was greatly accelerated. Methodist and Baptist missionaries arrived in covered wagons, drawn by oxen, in 1803. Cumberland Presbyterians came in 1811. And steadily there came homemakers from Tennessee, Kentucky, Virginia, and North Carolina.

In 1815 the United States Government surveyed the land between the St. Francis and the Arkansas Rivers in Arkansas, a tract which includes some of the Ozark country. Two million acres of this territory were set apart to be given as bounties to soldiers of the War of 1812. An old Arkansas history explains, "Thus the new territory from the start was peopled with the heroes of the war, men of courage and ability."

By 1817 there were 14,000 people in Arkansas. It became a territory in 1810 and a state in 1836.

John C. Campbell, in his book, *The Southern Highlander and His Homeland*, says,

"From 1830-1850 the westward migration from the Southern states received a new impetus. The decline of prices of cotton and tobacco in the south, together with the exhaustion of the soil, sent many thousands, including not only the poorer small farmers but planters caught by the general financial depression, to the northwest and southwest."

"Before 1850 Virginia had lost by emigration 26% of her native-born free inhabitants, South Carolina had lost 36% and North Carolina 31%. From 1831-40 Georgia gained nearly 34% in population, Alabama 91%, and Arkansas 275%. In the next decade, while the percentages of increase were lowered, the actual gain in population in these states was little less than in the preceding decade."

John C. Campbell, *The Southern Highlander and His Highland.* New York: Russell Sage Foundation.

W. V. Pooley, *Settlement in Illinois.* University of Wisconsin, 1908, quoted with the permission of the publisher.

Most of those who immigrated as far as Arkansas did not settle in the Ozarks but sought the lowlands farther south. But some, drawn irresistibly by the familiar lure of the highlands, and their ingrained love for forest-covered hills, followed the watercourses back into the beautiful mountains where there was hunting, fishing, pasturage, and land to till.

Watercourses were the highways at that time. Families which settled along the rivers and streams were on the main thoroughfares. Truly, passersby were rare and neighbors were few, but there was all the contact with others that the mountaineer desired. He was accustomed to solitude. He could not foresee that railroads and roads would replace the waterways as travel routes, and that these would not follow the rivers but would go across the mountains as directly as possible wherever they could not go around them.

After the streams ceased to be the primary lanes of travel, strangers seldom found their way into the hills. Before long, these few who did so were welcomed as long as they were transients, but the welcome vanished if there was any evidence that they hoped to stay as householders and neighbors. Communities had become fixed, and outsiders were not wanted. The mountaineers had an especial aversion to negroes. They were not tolerated in most localities, perhaps because of the highlanders' contempt for anyone who submits to servility. Consequently, people of other nationalities and races did not settle in the Ozarks. The result is that the mountain people today are direct descendants of the Anglo-Saxon colonists, unmixed with other strains.

Little did the early pioneer realize that his progeny would be isolated in this place which he chose for a home, separated from the outside world, perpetuating his customs and speech and beliefs. But this situation makes a study of them especially enlightening. In remote sections of the Ozarks the national background can be seen. There one can fill in the homely details of early American history, and make it real by watching the people, for their everyday life is a demonstration in the twentieth century of the life of the eighteenth. Their development was arrested soon after the time of the founding of the national government and they have remained dormant since, with scant cognizance of the changes that have taken place all around them, cut off as they are from a world that is unmindful of them and of which they are equally ignorant.

Their heritage is evidenced by many of the things which they have preserved. There are indications of their lineage in their architecture, their crafts, their economic life, and their superstitions. Marks of their Anglo-Saxon ancestry persist in their speech.

In what is probably the oldest piece of Anglo-Saxon poetry which has been preserved, supposedly written about 449 A. D., and known as *Widsit*, or the *Far Traveler*, one reads:

Widsit mapolade, wordhord *onleac*,
Widsit spoke, his word-hoard unlocked,

and it is reminiscent of the mountaineer's pronunciation of such words as "oncle" and "hongry."

He says "been" as though it were "ben."

"We-uns have ben right peart of late."

"I ben aimin' to ax you."

In the *Poema Morale*, written sometime between 1154 and the close of the twelfth century, the poet says:

Ich aem elder then ich wes a wintre and a lore;
Ic waelde more thanne ic dude, mi wit ah to *ben*
    more.

I am older than I was in winters and in lore;
I wield more than I did, my wit ought to be more.

And in about 1356 Sir John Mandeville in his *Travels* wrote:

There are many other countreys where I have not yet *ben* nor sene & therefore I can not speke properly of them.

"Peart" is found in Chaucer's *Canterbury Tales* (1386-1400). "Ax" is the primitive form of "ask."

"Hit" is not incorrect English. It is old English. It is the survival of the ancient Anglo-Saxon neuter of the pronoun "he" (hē, hēo, hit); and there is justification for saying "come" instead of "came."

"Hit jest come to me to do it that-a-way" is modern usage.

Hit com him on mode: & on his mern bonke.
bet he wolde of engle: ba aetelaen tellen.

It came into his mind, and his main thought,
That he would of the English the origins tell.

was written by Layamon in his *Brut* about 1225. And in 1362 Langland wrote the first version of his *Vision of William concerning Piers the Plowman* in which he says:

A-rys, and go reuerence godes resurreccioun,
And creop on kneos to the croys and cusse *hit* for a Iuwel,
And ryghtfullokest a relyk non riccher on erthe.
For godes blesside body *hit* bar for oure bote,
And *hit* a-fereth the feonde for such is the myghte,
May no grusliche gost glyde ther *hit* shadeweth!

The mountain woman explains, "Ye cain't hardly eat canned fruit *withouten* no sugar," and sometime between 1333 and 1352 Lawrence Minot wrote a ballad about Edward III which begins:

God, bat schope both se and sand,
Saue Edward, king of Ingland,
Both body, saul and life,
And grante him joy *withowten* strif.

Today is heard, "I'd jest as leave go but I'd lever have the kids stay to home." Chaucer, in describing the Clerk of Oxford, in his *Canterbury Tales*, said:

Him was *lever* have at his beddes heed
Twenty bokes, clad in blak or reed,
Of Aristotle and his philosophye,
Than robes riche, or fithele, or gay sautrye.

The woman who says, "My hosband, he holped to won the war," suggests Chaucer again.

The holy blisful martir for to seke,
That hem hath *holpen*, whan that they were seke.

The mountaineer's use of an "en" ending for a
verb is also warranted. He says, "I taken those
cheese to town," or "Her clothes air not fitten fer
school." Turn again to Chaucer:

And smale foules *maken* melodie,
That *slepen* alle night with open eye,
So priketh hem nature in hir corsages;
Than *longen* folk to gon on pilgrimages.

Double negatives, "Hit ain't no use a-tryin' to
plant nothin'," "Hit don't make me no difference,"
are reflections of an old turn of speech. There are
also double comparatives: "Seems like the hens
likes to set on the bed more better'n anywhere."

"They hain't got *nary* a quilt" is a corruption of
the old "ne'er a," as "ary" is of "e'er a."

A man may be "plumb crazy," but that use of
"plumb" is good Old English, as is the use of
"poke" to mean "sack."

There is a Scotch ring to "How kin I git yon
shote?"

The Old English sound of "We was wed jest before the war ceased. The baby was borned jest
after it ceaseded" fits oddly with the "hain'ts"
which these people have also inherited as a result
of their early American ancestors' contact with
Southern negroes, and with the "we-all" and "you-
all" from Kentucky and the "we-uns" and "you-
uns" of the Carolinas and Tennessee.

Some words that are thought of as peculiar to the

Appalachian mountaineer are found also in the Ozarks:

"Clarence wor a nice enough feller afore he wedded that Etta Hawkins an' took in her brood o' *feisty* brats. Etta she ain't nothin' but a *suggin*—pore white, ye mought say."

"Feisty" includes the ideas of frisky, mischievous, troublesome, and a general incorrigible nuisance. It is often used to describe a dog. In the Appalachians "suggin" means pouch, valise, or carry-all.

Vocabularies and pronunciations differ among localities and among individuals, in accordance with the degree of their exposure to outside influences.

Time has made changes in many words and meanings. Someone will say of a neighbor, "He's a purty lazy, *sorry* feller," without knowing that his word "sorry" has gone through a long process of evolution. Originally it meant, literally, "sore-y," covered with sores, a scabby knave, and it has gradually come to mean "good-for-nothing." The mountaineer will also say, "The crop, hit's ben moughty sorry this year."

A married woman is "Mis' " instead of "mistress" except in very formal speech, such as that used in a funeral sermon. A "narrow minded" person is one who is not very bright.

The effect of time and isolation are evident in the spellings and pronunciation and choice of names also. There are Dannels and Adkns and Adrons. One old couple will not agree on their name. She says it is "May," and he insists that it is "Mayse."

But then, she knows which furniture in their cabin and which stock in their field is "hern" and which is "hisn."

Various branches of a family will differ in the spelling of a name, as Knatcal and Knitchal, although they all pronounce it "Canitchal." Burrow is called Burr, although the former spelling persists. The name pronounced "Are-y" proves to be Ira. One is told to pronounce Dave Candy's name "like the state of Canady." Earl may spell his name "Irl."

Many old given names are in use, such as Laurie, Ezrie, Lorenzie, and Lonzo. But many relatives, bearing the favorite family names, live close by, families are large, and there has been no avenue for the inflow of more modern names from outside, so, for the sake of convenient differentiation, new names have been originated locally, such as Vennie, Orjal, and Clora.

Some families have given all the children names beginning with the same letter, as Albert, Algie, Addie, Arkie, and so on.

Some of the names are intriguing. Try repeating Bent Babb, or Please Waits, or Bown Downs. Then there is That Happel McSpadden with the "th" as in Theodore.

All consciousness of queer differences of names or speech is not one-sided. There is the mountain woman who complained that her neighbors had had visitors from Chicago, American visitors who "talked so comical we-uns couldn't make out what they-all was a-tryin' to say." And the miller who chuckled about some recent customers.

"Them two girls must of ben from town. They didn't know nothin'. I don't git much fer the millin', jest my grain toll, and that ain't much only it keeps us in corn pones. When I'd got done with grindin' their corn I hands it back to 'em.

" 'How much be it?' says one girl.

" 'I've tolled it aready,' s'I in my own homely way, thinkin' as how they had orter know.

" 'But how much do I owe you?' says she.

" 'I've already tolled it,' s'I agin.

" 'I never done heerd you. Who'd you tell?' says she. I thought I'd bust. I laughed fit to kill," and he burst out into hearty laughter again.

7

Personal Appearance

New moon, new moon, declare to me,
Shall I this night my true love see?
Not in his best, but in the array
As he walks in every day.

MOUNTAIN BABIES ARE LIKE BABIES THE WORLD
over, plump and sweet and the idols of their families. But soon they lose their baby roundness.
Mountain children are thin and long-legged and
pale. Their hair is light and dull.

As the girls reach adolescence they blossom;
their thin legs and arms fill out, their faces are
rounder and their complexions are often lovely.
They take more pains with their personal appearance at this age and are as attractive as girls anywhere. They usually marry very young and begin
the long strain of almost constant child bearing
and unceasing child care. They soon begin to fade
and wither. Their skin does not get flabby. It dries
and tightens over their faces and necks and hands.
They grow round-shouldered and hollow-chested
and flat-breasted. They make no attempt to retain
their figures. By the time they are fifty the women
are very old. Many do not live that long. And they
look old when they are thirty, though they may
still have sparkling young eyes and a ready smile.

The skinny little boys shoot up tall and lean. As they reach manhood they fill out until some of them are very fine looking. But they too, as years and the weight of family cares press upon them, grow hollow-cheeked and thin and stooped.

In a country of lank rawboned people whose leathery skin pulls tight over their cheek bones, a fat person is an oddity. Here the occasional round face and plump hands are likely to be flabby with an unnatural fatness which bodes no good for their possessor.

The children do not have "boughten clothes." The tiny baby's diapers and slips may be made of flour sacks, his little stockings of salt sacks. After the first period of white clothes, both boys and girls wear Mother Hubbard aprons cut down from larger discarded clothing. Now the baby is at the age between diapers and panties, an age that many mountain babies go through.

By the time he is three the boy will probably graduate to overalls, which will be his typical dress for the rest of his life. When they become ragged they may serve to expose rather than to conceal his little body, as he wears nothing with them except, perhaps, a shirt. Little girls add bloomers and possibly a slip under their sleeveless or short-sleeved dresses.

The mountain women are wonders at conserving every usable scrap of cloth. One will explain, "I ben makin' bloomers fer the little girls out of some of Tom's old shirt tails [you can imagine them; a dull, heavy, scratchy stuff] and I made 'em some princess slips out of some old ones of their gran'-

Farm Security Administration photograph by Rothstein

Mountain children

Farm Security Administration photograph by Shahn
Beltless print dresses

maw's. I had to cut up one of my dresser scarves this mornin' to make some diapers fer the baby. I felt right bad about ruinatin' it, but it had ben so long sence we'd got any flour sacks I was clean out."

Flour sacks serve a multitude of needs. They make good sheets and pillowcases, they are acceptable for underclothing and nightclothes and babies' layettes, they make desirable curtains, and are the material for fancywork of all sorts. Worn clothing can be used for rags, but flour sacks are new material to be utilized for things of importance, without a scrap of waste.

In case of necessity a tow sack (burlap) may be used to make a dress.

The girls often array themselves in the extreme of fashion when they go out, thanks to the mail-order catalogs, which are very valuable sources of general information in mountain communities. It is not unusual to meet girls walking along the road in beach pajamas, bright-colored sandals, and floppy hats. They use cosmetics with more abandon than artistry. But this dressing-up is only for the public. At home they dress like their mothers.

The older women have neither the inclination nor the wherewithal for such "fixin's." They seldom use cosmetics. They wear practical print frocks, with skirts attached at the waistline, and modestly long and full. Sometimes these are beautifully made and carefully laundered, sometimes patched and mended with stitches so neat and with patterns so perfectly matched that it is difficult to realize that the cloth is not whole. More often they are shapeless and faded, and eventually snagged and beltless.

A woman's total wardrobe needs are simple. When her husband goes to town to do the year's "tradin' " her request for herself and her daughters may run something like this:

"We'll be mighty pleased to git a few dry goods. We kin make out if we kin jest git us a dress pattern around, fer me and the girls. They don't have but one change. And you might fetch along a bolt of muslin, if it don't make you no difference. We're needin' princess slips and bloomers and gowns. I'll sew 'em on my fingers. If you kin git us one suit of clothes around we kin make out middlin'." A dress pattern is enough print material for one dress.

In addition to these things they may need cotton hose, or shoes. A hat is nice but not necessary. A coat will last for years. Except on extremely cold or stormy days extra wraps are not worn. The people are so accustomed to meeting all kinds of weather with a minimum of clothing that they do not seem to notice the cold.

A man's clothing needs are simple too. He must have overalls, blue work shirts, heavy work shoes, and a large straw hat for protection from the sun. Some men have underwear, more do not. A gangling mountain youth may have an embarrassing time trying to pull the two sides of a split overall leg together to cover his bare leg when he is in the presence of a strange lady. They do not have pajamas or ties. A man may have an odd suit coat to wear over his work shirt and overalls when he dresses up, but a matched suit, a pair of suspenders, a "dress" shirt, black shoes, socks, and a tie are a sign of affluence among the mountaineers, and these people do not spend much for luxuries.

The clothing of the mountain boy may be laughed at when he goes to the city, but it is no more outlandish than that of the inexperienced city boy in the mountains. The city boy's shoes, which scuff easily on the stones of mountain trails, his wool clothing which snags on thorns and bushes along the way, his hat with brim too narrow to protect him effectively from the sun, are just as obviously out of place and far more inappropriate.

Notwithstanding the customary caricature of mountaineers, most of the men and women wear shoes a good deal of the time. The children ordinarily do not, except in cold weather or for dress occasions. When a girl reaches adolescence her mother may say, "Marcelene here needs shoes. She's gittin' too big to run barefoot." A boy affects shoes at about the same age. The makeshift foot coverings are sometimes most extraordinary. A large household has many pairs of shoes of various sizes and kinds. These may be picked up carelessly and put on without finicky discrimination but with startling results. One family was seen with the following assortment of foot coverings:

One of the boys had a child's shoe, much too large for him, on one foot, and on the other a woman's high-topped shoe with a spike heel and pointed toe. The spike heel was so badly run over that he walked almost on the side of his foot. One of his sisters was wearing the other of the pair of child's shoes. For her second foot she had a slipper about half long enough, slipped over her toes and tied on. The slipper heel was directly under the arch of her foot. The toes had been completely cut out of the shoes of one of the older boys, to make room for his growing feet. The mother wore rubber overshoes tied on with string, the man was wearing tennis shoes, and the youngest children were barefooted.

This case is, of course, extreme, but it is not unique. The assortment should not suggest a lack of presentable footwear. The attitude is, "Oh, them's all right fer around home. I'll save my better ones fer best."

A good many persons find little incentive to take much pains with the daily toilet in a country where torn clothing and unkempt hair have become so familiar that they are hardly noticed, where money for clothing is scarce, and where neighbors, if there are any, have already seen the members of the family in all conditions of dress, and under all sorts of circumstances. And there may not even be any neighbors around that day. So it seems better to save the good clothes for a visit or for expected company.

Many of the men shave only on Sunday, and have their hair cut infrequently, not by a barber but by someone at home.

The women's hair is usually colorless and lusterless and stringy. It probably is not washed all winter. There is a theory in the mountains that if you wash your hair in the winter, no matter how warm the day, "you'll ketch your death of cold, and git pneumony fever and die and go to Glory shore."

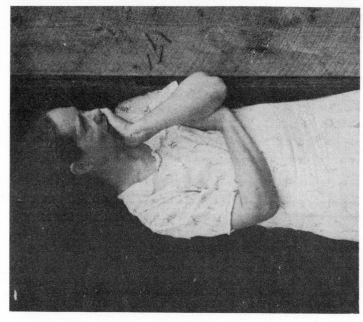

Farm Security Administration photograph by Shahn
Her hair in a neat knot

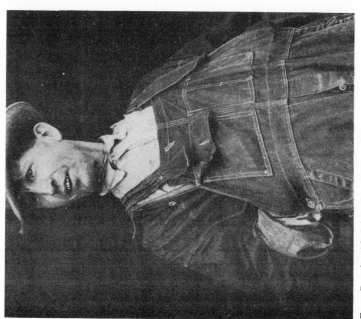

Farm Security Administration photograph by Shahn
A mountain man

Some people are deterred by this fear even in the summertime.

A few of the girls and some of their mothers get permanent waves. One may be had for a dollar and paid for in chickens, butter, eggs, or vegetables. Many put their hair up on curl papers or rags. Small kinks may be produced by either method. The older women pull their hair up into a neat knot, if they are inclined to be neat, or let it stick out of an untidy one, if they are untidy. There are few bobbed heads.

From lack of proper care and diet, and the use of snuff, the people's teeth grow yellow and decay. Then they are not filled but are extracted as soon as they give trouble, and are not replaced with false ones. As a result, all but the young people are apt to be snag-toothed.

So few persons do not have lips and teeth stained brown by tobacco, that a set of white teeth is noticeable. Tobacco juice shows in the wrinkles at the corners of the mouths of the older people as they talk.

Both men and women became experts at expectoration. The fireplace is the usual target. Brown stains around it give evidence that all have not yet reached the expert stage. There is one women who half rises from her chair in the midst of almost every sentence, makes a shot at a knothole in the floor five feet in front of her, and hits the bull's-eye every time. She is justly proud of her ability.

Many families raise and dry their tobacco, crumbling it as they need it. A few of the older men smoke it in foul-smelling pipes. Some old

women smoke corncob pipes. The men occasionally
buy cigarette tobacco in sacks and roll their own
cigarettes. A cigar is seldom seen in the mountains.

An old woman was telling about a revival meeting.

"They's two lady preachers down here from St.
Louis. The lead of their preachment is agin ter-
baccer. They're plumb fractious about it. They
claim as how they's folks'll walk ten mile fer the
'little brown devil.' I couldn't rightly say as to
that.

"I hain't never chewed the stuff," she claimed,
self-righteously, "but," her eyes twinkled, "I have
held a teeny mite in my cheek ever sence my first
gal was borned."

For the most part, the men chew plug tobacco
and the women dip snuff.

Did you ever see a woman use snuff? There are
two methods in vogue. Some women pull the lower
lip out into a V between the thumb and forefinger
and drop a little snuff into this trough. There it
lies, between lower lip and teeth, stimulating the
flow of saliva, gradually mixing with it, necessitat-
ing frequent spitting.

Other women prefer to use a snuff stick. From
a black gum tree they break a twig five or six
inches long and chew the end into a brush. This end
is dipped in snuff and placed well back in the side
of the cheek where it remains until the snuff is
gone, and the stick is removed to be dipped again.
Some women are seldom seen without a snuff stick.
They grow as proficient in talking around it as
some men are in manipulating the perpetual stogie.

Few of the women smoke anything. The idea of a woman smoking a cigarette shocks them tremendously. So does the idea of a "lady" drinking hard liquor. That is a masculine privilege.

8

Marriage

As Tommy Snooks and Bessy Brooks
Were walking out on Sunday;
Says Tommy Snooks to Bessy Brooks:
"Wilt marry me on Monday?"
To-morrow will be Monday.

MARRIAGE HERE, AS IN OTHER RURAL COMMUNITIES, is a necessary institution. Young people do not decide whether or not they want to get married—they only decide whom they want to marry. That they will marry is accepted as a foregone conclusion. No alternative occurs to them.

Boys marry as soon as they are old enough to get a place to farm. Girls are married very young. Though the true mountain girl, lacking the educational influence of both radio and magazine advertising, never heard of "B.O." nor of halitosis, she succeeds in getting and holding her man.

There are no big weddings in the hills. Many couples run away to be married. Their relatives and friends know that they expect to be wed but do not know when the event is to take place. The couple may go into town to be united by a justice of the peace. Or, if there is a minister in the neighborhood, they may go to him or to a minister in town. After the ceremony has been performed they will go together to their homes and tell their parents.

Some night soon after the wedding their friends will gather for a "chivari" (charivari). The revelers will not know that they are perpetuating an ancient custom of beating on pans and making hideous noises for the purpose of frightening evil spirits away from the new home. To them it will be only a gay occasion. And the newlyweds, expecting the surprise visit, will be prepared to feast the crowd.

If a partner dies, neither a man nor a woman is likely to remain long unmarried.

It is hard for a mountain man to farm without a woman's help, especially if he has a brood of small children. To rise early, get the children dressed, prepare the morning meal, care for the stock, and then go to the field to work till noon; to come home to prepare and eat and clear away the noon meal, water the stock, and go back to the fields; and then to come in at sundown, care for the stock and do the milking, prepare the evening meal, and get the children to bed, is more than a one-man job, even without considering cleaning and laundry work and mending and nursing. A man needs a woman about the place.

It is true that the children learn to look out for themselves and for the younger children very early, which is a great aid when they are left motherless, but it helps with only a part of the problem. An older child must miss school if she has the care of younger children. She may cook and clean as she is able, but unless her mother had "learnt" her to make garments "on her fingers" the family will require "boughten" clothes, which are more expensive. In case of illness a more experienced nurse is needed. Is it any wonder that a father will find another woman soon?

Sometimes a man's need for a wife necessitates detailed explanation as to the make-up of the family. Mrs. Sanders explains, "I'm Jeff's third woman. Five of the kids is ourn. One he got by his second woman, and the oldest one was by his first woman."

Sometimes it leads to great discrepancy in ages. Old Elmer Sims is sixty-five and his wife is twenty-four. Some of her stepchildren are almost twice as old as she.

A woman left husbandless is no better off than a widower. A manless family has its own problems.

The widow Peel explains, "We was a-livin' in one of the best of Ary Magness's places and thought we was goin' to make it fine. But Roy took sick. He was sick eight months afore he died and that throwed us in pretty bad shape, and no sooner had we lost him than Ary told us we'd have to leave. He wanted to give the place to a bunch what had a man. We couldn't find nowhars to go to, so the men around here got together and raised this here house fer us."

"This here" is a one-room log cabin without a fireplace. It has no floor but the earth, but it is large and tightly roofed and chinked. Two windowless window openings are well screened, but the doorway has neither solid nor screen door.

"Mis' Magness gives us milk fer tendin' her

cows, and the neighbors gives us what jobs they kin, fer a mess of peas or a few molasses, but there ain't much work fer a woman and a bunch of kids and we're wonderin' how we're a-goin' to export ourselves."

There is not much opportunity for a woman to do any but her own work. Her neighbors do their own washing and cooking, sewing and quilting. She has perhaps a better chance of finding quilting than others of these jobs if she has a reputation for doing neat work, for a neighbor may prefer not to quilt the top she has pieced and be willing to give some corn meal or a slab of bacon, in order to be spared the trouble. But a woman cannot make a living for herself and her children that way.

Many widows move into a town when they are left alone. Mrs. Watkins says, "We was a-livin' in the bottoms. We used to git flooded out about once a year, and I didn't want to have to git the kids and the stock out when the water begin to come up, without no man around. And if one of the kids got sick out there I wouldn't of had nobody no more to run fer help. So I rented my place out and come to town. Maybe I kin find some work here. I have hopes of findin' some sewin' or quiltin'. I'm very good at pants, not braggin'."

A woman is probably safer in the mountains than in a city. Persons are well known. The weight of public opinion is heavy and serves as a major deterrent to unwelcome coercion. Then, too, men of low moral standards can find women of their own sort to "keep company with." There are a few such women in the hills, well known and sedulously ostracized by their neighbors, and there are more in towns.

The young unmarried mother and her child are not treated unkindly. It is taken for granted that she shall keep her child with her. Of course there is much gossip. And if the girl's relatives find out who the child's father is, there may be a shotgun wedding. Such marriages often become happy ones. If the father is not forced to marry the girl, someone else will marry her and take her child, later on. If she settles down and becomes a good wife and mother, she is accepted by the community, which lets bygones be bygones.

There is little separation or divorce. Outside the mountains economic independence is quite possible for either a man or a woman. The question of bread and butter is not a major deterrent to divorce. In the mountains a man needs a housekeeper and helper. A woman needs a man to do the heavy work. Either needs the other in order to farm successfully. Each is economically dependent upon the other.

If a woman says that her husband was a good-for-nothing who wouldn't work so she "run him off and he went back to his folks, which makes three in that house who won't work," there is a great likelihood that she also had parents to go to.

If a woman leaves her husband she has probably found another man to support her and run away with him.

It is probable that the most important reason for the stability of marriage in the mountains is affectional rather than economic, however. People do not want to separate. It may be difficult for a husband and wife who work in different offices, meet different problems and different people, to maintain similar interests. The mountain couple has no such problem. Their knowledge and their concerns are the same, their joys and their sorrows. They share in the responsibility and the satisfactions of creative work.

Each knows he is necessary to the attaining of their common goal. They labor side by side. They attend the same social functions. They go to church together. They share the same faith. They are thoroughly acquainted with one another. They have no reason to question the security or worth of their marriage.

Most mountain families are close-knit, devoted groups with high moral standards, keen family pride, and mutual satisfaction in one another.

There are exceptional cases of persons who prefer to live alone.

Clyde Sim's wife ran away four years ago, leaving him with four little sons. The oldest is now fourteen. The boys brag, "We ben batchin' it." The house looks like it. "Course we cain't do all what our ma used to do. We pick berries when they git ripe in the spring, but we have to eat 'em right then, 'cause we don't know how to put 'em up."

"The other kids all has mas," the youngest mourns, pressing his fist hard against his chin to keep it from quivering.

"But we're purty good at batchin', jest the same," the oldest comforts him.

Clyde Sims does not want another woman.

An occasional mountain woman doesn't want a
man about the place. One such independent and
self-sufficient person is the "breeches woman." Her
fame has spread beyond her immediate neighborhood. "I've never seed her, but they say she dresses
and smokes and—cusses like a man."

She lives in a wild and desolate country, far from
other houses. Her tiny one-room, windowless cabin
is set in a tangle of woods with the fenced barn lot,
without any barn, the only cleared space within
sight of the house. The walls inside the cabin are
hung with harness and straps and chains.

Minnie Cannon went to visit her one day. If she
had not known that a woman lived in this house
alone she would have thought it a man coming to
meet her. She wore a heavy blue work shirt and
overalls, heavy work shoes, and a man's felt hat.
Her coarse gray hair was cut short like a man's,
not a barbershop haircut, but the rough home haircut of the mountaineer. Her skin was like old
leather, and she was small and wiry. She trusted
Minnie and told her her story, which few of her
neighbors have heard, for she ordinarily keeps her
own counsel.

"A good many year back they found me a-layin'
on a street in town one day, sick with brain fever,
and they took me to the county farm to die. But 't
warn't my time, and I got on my feet agin in spite
of 'em. Then one of the doctors in town, he doctored
on me and directly he give me an operation. After
I got over that I decided I'd be better off if I went
out on my own. So I found this homestead land and
come out here and built me a house, and home-

Farm Security Administration photograph by Shahn   Husband and wife—partners

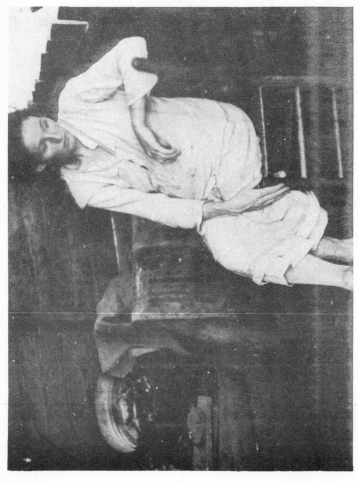

Farm Security Administration photograph by Shahn

Wouldn't give 'em up if you could help it

steaded eighty acres. Hit's ben mine fer many a year."

"You mean you built it your lone self?" Minnie asked.

"Yes, ma'm. Every last bit of it. I cut down my own trees and trimmed the logs. I split my own boards, and I raised it and chinked it and covered it my own self.

"I ain't ben into town fer years. I git some neighbor to do my tradin'. Sence my operation I cain't stand nothin' tight around my waist, it makes me sick to my stomach, so I started wearin' man's clothes—in 1911 that was—and I don't like to go into town in 'em. But they're better anyhow. They don't snag in the bresh like a print dress.

"I got me a horse (he's most too old to work now), and we cleared twenty or twenty-five acre and put in ten fifteen acre every year. I raise and butcher my own meat."

Minnie was sitting on the one chair, just inside the cabin, and her hostess sat on the doorstep, rolling and smoking one cigarette after another. The papers she used were thick and yellow. Her tobacco was in a little bag. She is one of the few women in the hills who smokes cigarettes and, judging by the smell of the pungent black smoke, hers would knock out a strong man.

"Don't you ever git scairt away back here?" Minnie asked.

"Not often. The snakes used to fret me at first when I'd come home and find one a-stickin' its ugly green head out'n my bed, or see a long black one a-hangin' from the rafters in the light of the lamp at night. But I got so I could kill 'em good and I know now that most of 'em wouldn't hurt me nohow. I'm kinda leary of a copperhead or a rattler yit, but the rest I don't mind.

"I'd more ruther live right here by myself than anywheres I know. And I shore don't want no man botherin' around me. I had one once. They's them as come snoopin' around actin' sweet now and then, but I git shet of 'em purty quick. I'd ruther be my own boss."

"I know. I run one off, too," Minnie confided.

9

Children

Dance a baby, diddy,
What can mammy do wid'e?
But sit in a lap,
And give 'un a pap,
Sing dance a baby, diddy.

IT WAS A BEAUTIFUL SPRING AFTERNOON, BUT
young Mrs. Wilson had no eye for beauty. Her
eyes were turned down the road, and in them was
intense anxiety. It had been necessary for her
husband to go into town. She "was expectin' " any
time now. Suppose her time should come while he
was gone and there was no one to go for help!

Her first born, a two-year-old, would be of little
use. She had no near neighbor. Her need had been
too uncertain for her to ask anyone to come from
a distance. The only telephone in the vicinity was
in a hamlet several miles away and it had been out
of order for three weeks.

Mr. Wilson finally arrived, his hard-pushed team
exhausted because of his anxiety to reach home.
His relief at finding his wife still safe made him
forget his own exhaustion. He would not leave her
again until time for her to "bring forth her little
baby." Then he would go for relatives to help him
care for her and "it."

Some mothers are never attended by a physician; others may be for the first child or two. Then they are considered experienced enough to dispense with his services, and have only the help of some self-made local midwife, or a neighbor who knows what is to be done because she has had children of her own.

The need for prenatal examination and care is undreamed of. Many of a doctor's country maternity calls come to him as a complete surprise. There has been no warning and no prearrangement. There are expectant mothers with elephantine legs suggestive of uremia, who will not consult a doctor because the last baby has not been paid for "and hit's goin' to be bad enough to send fer him when the time comes," or who think that such a swelling is a natural part of the process; and there are other mothers, "the time" now past, suffering with milk leg. It is no wonder that the maternity and infant mortality rates are appallingly high, not in the areas of Arkansas where births are registered, but in the hill districts where only about 40 per cent of births or deaths are recorded.

There are some things which a mother can do for her coming baby, which, she has been told, are far more important than conferring with a doctor. If she fails in these things, irreparable ill may result. A wise woman curbs her craving for certain foods during pregnancy, for if she is intemperate in satisfying a desire for a particular food, her child may bear a mark resembling it. There are birthmarks the shape of strawberries, pears, and other edibles to prove the validity of this theory. She tries not to see anything frightening or repulsive—a snake or a ferocious animal, for instance— for the baby may be marked with the likeness of that thing. If she unavoidably sees or hears something which causes her acute terror or horror, the result may be far more serious than the acquisition of an unsightly birthmark. Her unfortunate experience may frighten the wits out of her child and he may be born an idiot—"a pore half-wit"—"if he don't die a-bornin'."

On the other hand, if, during pregnancy, she can avoid or be protected from all excess and all unpleasantness, and if she is sweet and affable, the fortunate baby may be blessed with a pleasant, happy disposition.

A mother will sometimes stay in bed for nearly a week after the birth of her first child, or longer, if there are complications. At the end of two weeks she will be doing her own scrubbing and washing. But a mother of experience takes out scarcely any time at all. After two or three days in bed she will begin to go about her usual duties again.

Not long ago a mountain woman, whose husband had recently been sent to the veteran's hospital at Fayetteville, came jolting into town in a wagon with a neighbor family for some needed groceries for herself and her six children. The children were too young to make the trip for her. The wagon drew up to a filling station on Main Street, and the two women climbed down and went into the rest room. A few minutes later the neighbor came out alone to announce to the astonished attendant that his station was the birthplace of a baby boy.

The proprietor had prided himself on operating a station which offered a wide variety of services, but this was going too far. He telephoned desperately for a doctor and the county nurse. They arrived in a few minutes, to find mother and child doing nicely. They moved them to the doctor's office where the woman could lie down. There was some delay in securing the services of a volunteer motorist to take the mother and baby to their home. They did not get started until late afternoon, and it is reported that the mother urged that arrangements be completed as quickly as possible in order that she might get there in time to do the milking.

It sometimes seems as though all the married women in the Ozarks, except the very old, are either expectant or nursing mothers. Perhaps it only seems that way because the pregnant women always mention their need of a layette, and the nursing women always take advantage of a visit to feed the baby.

A baby is ordinarily breast fed until superseded by the next baby. Sometimes a successor does not appear to "put his nose out of joint" for a year or two, and the last child of a family, having no competition, may continue to nurse until he is two or three years old. A small child will walk up to his mother, pull her dress down and help himself to a between-meal drink without seeming to attract her attention. But for a child of that age the milk is supplementary, for, from the time he was old enough to reach for the food served at the family table, he will have been on a heavy adult diet, including coffee.

One favorite pacifier for a little child is a bacon rind. He sucks it until he tires of it and then puts it down in any convenient spot, as he goes about his play. Later he returns to it and sucks it again unless the dog has done away with it in the meantime. Little tots may play on the floor with a cold biscuit until its original color is quite disguised, before devouring it.

The children are ingenious in inventing playthings and games. A gourd is a durable rattle for a baby. A stick makes an admirable horse. A doll made of rags or yarn may be very dearly loved. Many happy hours may be spent in a playhouse outlined on the ground with rocks and roofed by a great tree. If a ball is lacking, a beanbag can be almost as much fun. A boy can become an expert marksman with a slingshot made of a forked stick and a bit of inner tube.

Animals are great playmates, particularly when they are young. Little pigs, chicks, colts, and calves, as well as kittens and puppies, give special delight to the youngsters. Wild creatures, too—birds and squirrels and rabbits—are of interest to them.

The children spend much time with their parents. They play close by as their mother washes or irons or bakes. They watch their father as he plows and plants and reaps. They follow along at feeding and milking and egg-gathering time, and they are on hand for butchering and canning. Eager to be "grown up," they beg to help and gradually they are taught the home tasks by their parents.

It is possible that mountain children get more real pleasure and excitement from their simple playthings and their creative play than is afforded many children who are satiated with an abundance of toys and games and deprived of close comradeship with adults.

As would be expected in a land where knowledge of sanitation and prevention are deficient, illness among the children is frequent. Croup and convulsions and summer complaint, that scourge of the dread second summer, are all too familiar to the mountain mother, but they are none the less terrifying. They strike suddenly and are quickly over.

The baby's sleep is restless—a baby with golden curls. Her cheeks are flushed with fever, and her eyes are but half closed. Each time she stirs, fretting, either the mother or the father, who seems as gentle as a woman, is there beside her to pat her and croon soothingly, "There, there, sugar. Hit is all right."

Feverishly the parents work there in their little cabin, alone and far from help, trying all the treatments which the mother can remember, brewing concoctions which have been taught her by her mother—who raised ten and only lost five—using lard and herbs and other home remedies in a desperate effort to stay the illness before it requires of them another farewell and leaves them, in place of their precious baby, only another little mound in the distant graveyard.

Farm Security Administration photograph by Shahn
Mother and child

Farm Security Administration photograph by Shahn
Beloved playthings

Suppose the baby dies. It is better so, you say? The baby has been spared the hardship and suffering of growing up in an impoverished mountain home, and the family is left with one less mouth to feed. Mountain parents do not feel this way about it. As Mrs. Richardson said, "No matter how many kids a body has, you wouldn't give 'em up, once they're here"—if you could help it. But so often they cannot.

When a baby has gone, there is soon another to take its place in the family, though never in the heart of its mother. There will only be a little longer jump in the stairsteps of the children's height to show that one step is missing. For, in the average mountain family, the children come with regularity, as long as the woman is able to bear them.

Except in times of crop failure or depression, when twelve continue to eat almost six times as much as two, a big family is an asset. One man, whose wife has presented him with only one child, complains, "We cain't git nor keep no good place to farm, fer jest the three of us cain't tend as much land as a big family kin, so we allers gits run out by a bigger bunch."

The larger the family the better chance there is that the production will exceed the consumption. Each child more than pays for himself.

So much for the economic side of the problem. There is no awareness of an eugenic problem. Neither is there concern for the mother's health. Was it not intended that women should bear children? Any desire to limit the number or frequency of births, or at least any mention of such a desire, is revolutionary and radically unconventional.

In spite of the fecundity of the mountain mother, there is one credulous little woman whom it would be difficult to convince that her town sisters do not know a secret of which her mountain neighbors are unaware.

She is the little "Hello Woman," so called in town because when she comes in each week with eggs and chickens to sell, peddling them around to the houses instead of selling them more cheaply to a grocery merchant, she follows the mountain custom of standing at the door and shouting, "Hello," until someone comes. Doorbells are outside her experience, and she does not care to try them.

She walks down the sidewalk, stopping at each house, while her faithful horse pulls her little cart down the street, keeping up with her.

For the last twenty-five years she must have saved the same costume exclusively for her trips to town—high-heeled, high-topped, black laced shoes, a full black skirt gathered into a wide band at the waist, a tight basquelike waist with long sleeves and high neck, and a sunbonnet.

She stopped one day at a house where two little cousins were playing in the yard. When the mother of one of them came to the door the little "Hello Woman" asked, indicating the children, "Them be twins, ain't they?"

"Oh, no," was the answer. "There's three months difference in their ages."

"Land alive, honey!" exclaimed the little woman. "I didn't know it could be done that-a-way!"

10

Education

Oh that I was where I would be,
Then would I be where I am not.
But where I am I must be,
And where I would be I cannot.

THE SOUND OF A BELL REACHED A BOY RIDING DOWN
a mountain road. He urged his mule to greater
speed until he came to a log schoolhouse set in a
clearing in the woods. At the door stood a girl
ringing a hand bell. Children carrying lunch
buckets were scurrying to her from all directions.
Several saddle horses were tied to trees. A wagon
came bumping down the road, bringing more
children.

The boy hobbled his mule and went to the schoolhouse. It was a one-room building. There were windows in the two side walls, but there was little glass
in them. Window lights may be replaced promptly
for a time after a school building is first constructed, but after a year or two the school board decides
that if the boys will persist in breaking the glass
out as soon as it is put in, it may be just as well not
to hurry to replace it, so the window frames are
left empty for longer periods thereafter.

At the two back corners of the clearing stood
two toilets, their doorways unprotected by lattice-

work or shrubbery or any sort of shelter. Sometimes there is only one and sometimes none.

The young teacher led her class into the schoolroom. On the wall near the door were pegs for the wraps. The wall at the opposite end of the room was unbroken. On it hung a small strip of blackboard. In front of it were the teacher's desk and chair. This was the limit of her equipment.

The children sat on long homemade benches before homemade desks.

A large wood stove was set near the center of the room for the winter term, with logs and kindling wood piled high against a wall near by. The children seated near the stove are hot, and those in the corners or near the open windows are cold on cold or stormy days.

One of the older boys handed the teacher a note. "Kerseys ast me to give you this here when I come by their place this mornin'," he explained. She directed the children in beginning their work. Then as they studied she read it.

"Dere teacher, the Cumins has to littel children older nuff to go to school. They havin no Books. They want to school ther kids but they have ran out a ther Books an coudnt by no more this term. I thank they need help if iny one does. It is nesery."

She turned to the boy who was waiting for her answer. "The Kerseys must not have heard that the state is furnishing school books now. You tell them," she instructed the boy, "and tell the Cummings children to come on and go to school."

Until recently the necessity for purchasing

their own books has been a major deterrent to
school attendance for many.

A minimum number of books is needed, for there
is no attempt at any sort of vocational training in
the smaller schools. As many of the children do not
continue in school long, it is necessary that the
most essential of the rudiments of education be
given first. Even if a boy continues his attendance
for eight years (during the five or five and a half
months that he can attend each year), with his
teacher's time divided each day among the entire
work of seven other grades besides his own, there
is not much time for such "foolishments" as cooking or sewing or carpentry or even citizenship. If
he can read and write and do "enough cipherin' to
do his tradin'," he can manage. If he gets some
geography and history in addition, he is just that
much better off.

Few mountain children get more than this
minimum, for about 65 per cent of all the schools
are one-room schools, with all the grades meeting
in one room, with only one teacher. These one-
room schools have an average enrollment of about
fifty. Another 20 per cent of the schools have two
rooms with an average attendance of one hundred
to be divided and taught by two teachers. The
limited funds available prohibit any adequate provision of buildings.

There has been some attempt at consolidation
of mountain school districts to provide, with the
combined funds, suitable and properly equipped
buildings and better-trained staffs. This is an admirable arrangement for sections bordering on

good highways, but in parts of the hills which are not honeycombed with all-weather roads, such combinations are infeasible.

At present, in the remoter regions, the schools are scattered, and the children are scattered more. Roads are poor or nonexistent. Children may have to walk or ride horseback across several miles of mountains to reach a one-room school. Some cannot reach one at all.

Even where transportation is provided there is, at present, another obstacle to consolidation. Recently a plan was instituted in one locality for bringing the children who lived within walking distance of the highway, into the town by bus for their education. A plausible objection to this plan, offered by some parents, was that the clothing which was suitable for attendance at the little one-room country schoolhouse was laughed at in town, and they could afford no better.

Some cannot afford even that good enough for the local school. When a poverty-stricken family's crop is made, the children will chop or pick cotton for a neighbor, to earn money for school clothing, if they can find a neighbor who can pay them cash. If not, they will have to stay at home if their father cannot buy them the extra clothing. Children can live at home in clothes "not fitten fer school," and they can live at home without warm coats or hats or shoes.

Illness is another factor in poor attendance. Epidemics are frequent and widespread. And a child who may have no disease and who might feel well enough to walk to a building near by, or to ride to one farther away, may not feel like a walk of several miles.

Children are seldom kept home from school to work, for the terms have been arranged to avoid special work seasons.

Ground is broken for gardens in late January, and onions and lettuce and radishes and mustard will be planted in February unless the spring is unusually late. In March planting of the kitchen garden will be completed, and the ground will be prepared for the main crops which will be planted in April. Corn is hoed and cotton is chopped in June and July. Both hoeing and chopping are done with a regular garden hoe. Both words mean weeding and thinning after the young shoots are several inches high. During late July and August the corn and cotton need less attention, but by September cotton picking may be started. The heaviest part of that will be finished by the end of October, though some may still be left until nearly Christmas time.

Now for the effect on education. The children may go between November and March, but in March the schools are closed in order that the children may help, during April, May, and June, with the planting and chopping. Then there is a summer term during July and August while the crops are growing, but the children are dismissed again from late August until November so that they may pick cotton.

All schools do not meet from November till March and during July and August. Most of them have some summer term, but the average number

of school days in the Ozark country is about 110,
or five and a half months a year. More days would
cost more money.

Most families want their children to "git some
book larnin'." Occasionally the attitude is met, "I
got along all right without no schoolin' and my kids
kin too. I need 'em at home." Occasionally the
plea is made, "My kids cain't go to school 'cause
they hain't got no schoolin' clothes," and then when
the necessary clothing is supplied the children still
are absent. But in most cases the inaccessibility of
a school, illness, or the lack of suitable clothing, is
necessary to prevent attendance. These factors are
keeping more than 25 per cent of the mountain
children away, and an omnipresent truant officer
couldn't make them go.

As the agricultural system affects the time of
school terms, and poverty is responsible for inadequate equipment and the short school year, so the
economic stringency of the hills also limits the
choice of teachers. The salary of the teacher of the
one-room school averages about forty dollars a
month during the term. The teacher in the two-
room school may receive about sixty dollars. Not
many college graduates will teach in a public school
for forty dollars a month, or an annual total of
perhaps two hundred dollars. If a girl with an
A.B. degree cannot get a high-school position, she
will take a course in shorthand and typewriting, or
in beauty culture, in the hope of earning more.

Consequently, 10 per cent of the Ozark mountain
teachers have had no high-school training whatever. Seventy per cent have had nothing above

A one-room school

Wall and door of most interesting pictures

high school, and another 10 per cent have attended a college for only two years. The final 10 per cent have had more than two years of college work. These are teaching in the high schools in the towns.

Most of the boys and girls of the mountains are getting all of the schooling they will ever get from teachers who have had only a high-school education or less, and who, culturally, have the same background as their students. For fewer than 10 per cent of the hill country children go on to high school.

Even these teachers might be easier to keep with the two or three hundred dollars a year promised them, if they were sure of being paid in cash. If a district gets behind with its salaries it will pay in script instead of cash. These teachers' warrants are promises to pay when the district can collect the cash in taxes. Some districts have issued so many warrants that it will take years to redeem them at the present rate of taxation, and land taxes in Arkansas are comparatively high now.

Most teachers have to manage on very little money. Some member of the school board will perhaps give the teacher her board and room in his home, in lieu of part of her salary. And some woman will do her washing in return for music lessons for a child, and so she will contrive to live.

Compared with more prosperous parts of our country, the educational preparation of the mountain children is very inferior, but most of them are getting far more training than their parents had.

Many of the older people have had little or no formal education. Illiteracy is extensive. Men, unable to write so much as their own names, must mark an X on papers requiring their signature. And even the X's are crooked, like a small child's, so unaccustomed are their fingers to the feel of a pencil. When it is necessary to know how many acres of land are owned by a family, an old tax receipt may be dug out of a trunk and turned over to one who can read, to find the answer. When a parent is asked the ages of the children, an old notebook may be handed out, in which some more literate friend has recorded the names and dates of birth. And sometimes when a mother is asked how many children she has, she will answer, "I cain't rightly tell you straight off but I kin call their names and you kin count 'em up." When the spelling of an unusual name is requested the response often is, "Hit don't make me no difference. Spell it jest as you like." And any suggested spelling is repeated, with an evident desire to fix it in mind. When Dowell Williams' wife was asked how to spell her husband's first name she was embarrassed. "I spell it D-w-l, fer short. You kin spell it however you like."

Some of the more ambitious and persevering older people have increased their reading ability, after their few early days at school, by labored conning of the Bible or of mail-order catalogs, or by perusal of occasional journals which have come into their hands. Secondhand magazines are highly prized, studied over until they are learned by heart, and then preserved as wallpaper, with the most interesting pictures or reading matter turned toward the room. The more prosperous may even

subscribe for a farm magazine or a weekly news-
paper. A daily paper is almost unknown in the
mountains.

But the bulk of knowledge has been handed down
by word of mouth from one generation to the next,
with consequent decrease and distortion of facts.
In the spring the little school held its graduation
exercises. Everyone from far and near came;
whole families in wagons, riding in chairs set in the
wagon bed or seated in the back of the wagon with
their feet hanging out; individuals on horseback;
and groups walking the dusty road together.

The event was so largely attended that the crowd
overflowed the seats and aisles and window sills,
and many had to stand in the yard, looking in.

Lamps set on brackets around the room threw a
yellow, wavering light. One of them was pouring
out smoke.

Before the opening of the program the whole
room was filled with a buzz of whispering like the
buzz of angry bees. The noise subsided with the
beginning of the exercises. The audience enjoyed
the choruses sung by the boys and girls. They were
quiet for a humorous reading. The parents of each
student listened while he gave his "oration." But
when the imported speaker of the evening began
his address a low hum was discernible, mounting in
rapid crescendo to the intensity of the previous
buzz, punctuated by a baby's wail or a grand-
father's snore. These people did not come to listen
to incomprehensible eloquence from the platform.
They came to hear the singin', see the young-uns
graduate, and renew old acquaintances.

11

Family Life

The cat was asleep by the side of the fire,
The mistress snored loud as a pig;
Jack took up his fiddle by Jenny's desire,
And struck up a bit of a jig.

LIFE, FUNDAMENTALLY, CONSISTS IN BEING BORN, maintaining physical existence, bearing and rearing offspring, and dying.

In modern society this skeleton is so well padded and clothed that we are not conscious of it. For many, the maintenance of life does not require great or continuous struggle. The earning of bread is not completely absorbing. The individual does not have merely enough to sustain life, but has it in more or less abundance. Birth is eased by science. The responsibility of the home for rearing children is shared by a number of social institutions—the school, the church, and other youth-guidance and character-building organizations. Death is deferred and assuaged. There is time for activities not necessitated by life's fundamentals—activities either self-centered or altruistic. Often the framework is so well concealed that these other things seem most important.

It is not so in the mountains. Life there is much closer to the unadorned skeleton. Many of the embellishments are lacking. The struggle to maintain life begins at birth and ends with death, with no comfortable surplus. The bearing of offspring is dangerous and unalleviated. Almost the entire responsibility for rearing the young rests upon the home. Rarely is death delayed by medical science and rarely is its pain relieved.

But the mountaineer is not oppressed by any such morbid conception of his existence. A man seldom looks at his own life in outline. Since he cannot foresee the future he wastes but a small portion of his thought in wonder about it. How fortunate it is that he cannot see ahead! Foreknowledge would dull his joys when they came and oppress him with dread of his sorrows.

He spends little time in looking back, except in event of bereavement or some other upheaval which changes the course of his life and sets off the part that is gone from that to come. In retrospect the edge has worn off past sorrows and the excitement from past joys.

It is an observer who sees a life diagramatically. The man who is living it sees it as a composite of little things. He is too close to them to see its broader aspects. Its drabness is dimmed for him because of his interest in things of the moment, and his plans enliven it.

An observer sees a mountaineer's day in the abstract, as getting up early, working hard, and dropping into an uncomfortable bed, tired out, at night. The mountaineer sees the same day, as getting up a little earlier than usual to finish a bit of fencing uncompleted the day before, finding the first blade of corn pushed through the earth, discovering a hidden hen's nest, ministering to a sick cow, catching the little pigs that escaped when the sow rooted a way for them under the pen, getting the chores done before dark, speculating on the chance of rain tomorrow, being pleased with an especially tender bit of salt pork for supper and, finally, enjoying sound sleep in a bed made comfortable, not by an inner-spring mattress, but by hard work and long inurement—a busy day full of interests and irritations and satisfactions, ending with rest well earned. Such is life in the concrete.

Someone has said, "The poverty, with dignity, and composure of the mountain people are so unlike the customary American attitude that to see the people in their homes is to remember them forever."

Little Anne Carter went out from town to spend the day with John and Sarah Brogdon and their ten children. It was a busy day in the cotton-picking season.

Before Anne arrived John and the boys had completed the morning chores, and the family had finished the breakfast prepared by Sarah and the girls.

John and his older sons climbed into the wagon and drove away to the field where they were to pick that day. Sarah and the girls stayed to wash the breakfast dishes and set bread for the evening meal.

Sarah sifted some flour into a bowl and poured water over it. In answer to Anne's question, she explained, "I'm startin' some east (yeast). It has to set till it's worked good. I like east made with taters better, but I'm plumb out."

The yeast for the light bread is almost always homemade, and the bread is usually very dark and heavy. Biscuits, made three inches in diameter, often look more appetizing. They are ordinarily made with sour milk and soda. Baking-powder and sweet-milk biscuits are rare.

When the necessary morning work was done Sarah set the baby on her hip and she and the older girls started for the cotton field. Joey, aged two, was too young to be of any use in the field, so nine-year-old Mary was left at home to care for him and the fire, and to prepare the noon meal for the family.

Upon arriving at the field, Sarah put the baby down in a corner and left four-year-old Sally and Anne to watch him. Since he was still nursing he had to be accessible when he got hungry. Mountain babies are fed when they cry, rather than on schedule.

Sally showed Anne how to make delightful dresses and hats of pawpaw leaves, pinned together with long locust thorns. Soon both little girls were happily engaged in the construction of new wardrobes.

As they worked Sally taught Anne a song. It was a long "ballit," but Sally knew it all because she had heard it sung countless times during her short life and it was her favorite. It went like this:

Mr. Frog went courting, he did ride
Pistol and sword upon his side,
Rode up to Miss Mouse's door,

Said, "Miss Mouse, are you within?"
"Yes, kind sir, I sit and spin."

CHORUS

Kimo, kimo—delto—karo,
Bob sing to my Rato kimo.

Mr. Rat went in and took Miss Mouse upon his knee,
Said, "Miss Mouse, will you marry me?"
"I cannot answer that so well
Until I do my uncle tell."

CHORUS

When Uncle Rat now came home,
Said, "Who's been here since I've been gone?"
"A very fine gentleman, here has been,
And asked me for to marry him."

CHORUS

Then Uncle Rat went to town
For to buy his niece a wedding gown.
"Where shall the wedding supper be?"
"Way down yonder in a hollow tree."
"What shall the wedding supper be?"
"Two blue beans and a black-eye pea."

CHORUS

First came in a little moth
For to lay the table cloth.
Then there came a little bug
With him brought a little brown jug.
Also there was a bumble bee
With a banjo on his knee.

Solemnly walked the Parson Rook,
Under his arm a very large book.
The owl did hoot, the birds, they sang,
And through the woods the music rang.*

---

* A contribution by Miss Phoebe Park to the book, *Folklore of
Romantic Arkansas*, by Fred W. Allsopp (Kansas City: The Grolier
Society).

Resting while the cotton sack is weighed

Washing facilities

The rest of the family—father, mother, and the
other six children, from fifteen-year-old Jack to
five-year-old Luther—worked in the field. The cotton which was ready must be picked quickly, so all
hands were needed.

Luther was too small to pull the heavy cotton
sack alone. An older brother helped him with it.
The duck cotton sacks are made in three sizes—six,
seven and a half, and nine feet long. They are
pulled along the ground by a strap slung over one
shoulder. The largest size, to be used by a man,
will hold a hundred and fifty pounds of cotton, the
woman's size holds one hundred pounds, and the
child's seventy-five pounds.

Almost as soon as a child is old enough to walk
he is a helper. The little fellows can do weeding
and drop seeds, and pick a little cotton.

Arkansas was the first state to ratify the national child-labor amendment to the federal con-
stitution, yet the children of her mountains work
from the time they are large enough to pull weeds
or hoe or pull a cotton sack.

It is difficult to keep a man from "lettin' his own
kids do a little weedin' now and then." With the
methods and equipment used at present, a man
working his farm alone could not possibly cultivate
as much land as he can when the other eight or nine
members of his family are working with him, and
the whole family working together is scarcely able
to fend off starvation now.

Being less help than the others, Luther was the
one chosen to bring a bucket of cool water to the
workers in midmorning.

The wagon was left in the field at noon, and they all walked back to the house. John Brogdon led the way. Suddenly he stopped, pointing to a spot on the ground a few feet ahead.

"Did you ever see one of them things?" he asked Anne.

She could distinguish nothing at first, but a slight movement showed her a coiled snake, almost the color of the dry weeds on which it lay.

"That there's a puff adder. He's pizen. See him puff his head out at us?" These snakes are harmless, but many mountaineers believe them to be poisonous. Mr. Brogdon broke a long switch from a near-by bush and began to lash the snake. It stretched out straight on the ground and he beat it from one end to the other.

"Never try to kill one of 'em straight off with a rock or a club," he admonished. "Always git you a switch and switch it. If you try the other way and miss it, it'll strike you shore, but when you switch it it sorter stuns it and gives you time to kill it careful."

When the snake was dead he stopped switching. "Hit'll twitch till sundown," he told Anne.

Again they went on their way, watching the grass around them carefully.

Again John stalked ahead, as is the custom of the mountain man. When couples walk thus in town, the woman two steps behind the man and he talking back over his shoulder to her, he appears arrogant and ill-bred. Actually the custom is the essence of chivalry. Mountain paths are single width, and possible danger lurks always ahead.

As they went along John bragged to Anne about his wife.

"Ever sence we was wed, whenever I heerd of a job of work, I could go git it and leave Sarie do the plowin' or whatever's to be done that day. She's a good hand with a team."

"That ain't nothin'," said Sarah modestly. "Look at Lucy Richardson—her with the new house. You recollect her draggin' foot? And she picks cotton! She kin pick a right smart lot in a day, goin' along between the rows on her knees. She 'lows it makes 'em right sore when she first starts out each year, but she gits used to it later. If I was that-a-way I'd reckon I was doin' a-plenty to tend a house and kids, let alone workin' in the field."

Margetta, the oldest daughter, brought a splint-bottomed chair to the little front porch for Anne. The day was warm, and there was a little breeze there which she was to enjoy while the meal was being "served up" and the others were taking their turns at the washpan and comb and bit of mirror at the front door.

The afternoon was a repetition of the morning.

When the family returned from the field they rode in the wagon which was piled up with cotton. This was unloaded onto the front porch, for safe keeping.

The men did the evening chores while the women prepared the meal. After supper the men sat in the yard while the women cleared the meal away. Anne's parents took her home, and the Brogdons all went to bed. A cotton-picking day was over.

Their evening meal had consisted of fried ham,

yams, several other late-garden vegetables, light bread, coffee, and apple pie baked the day before. All but the baby ate some of everything.

In this country of cows and chickens and gardens and sunshine, "plagery" (pellagra) and rickets are prevalent. Much of the milk is fed to the pigs rather than to the children, while the children drink thick black coffee. Eggs are saved for tradin' at one of the stores in town or with a peddler. There are peddlers who go periodically to remote places in the mountains, carrying pots and pans, plain cotton materials, threads and other notions, and some medicines, which they trade for poultry and eggs.

A "pat o' butter" is made only for special occasions. There is no refrigeration to keep it fresh and sweet. Such things are kept moderately cool by being let down into the well or set in a springhouse or in a box in the creek, but this preserves them only temporarily.

Meat spoils quickly. The choicest lean pieces are eaten fresh on the day of the butchering. The rest must be cured. The preserved lean meat is eaten next. Eventually all but the fat salt meat is gone. This may be the only sort of meat in the diet for months.

In the spring in the fields there are poke and dandelion and mustard greens. There is an abundance of fresh vegetables from the kitchen garden all summer—radishes and onions, lettuce, spinach, and carrots, turnips and beets and their tops, peas, beans, and okra, potatoes, tomatoes, and cabbages —and from the fields, peanuts and corn. Sweet

The peddler's truck

A springhouse

Ready for work

corn is not raised here. The family, as well as the stock, eats field corn.

But in the winter the story is different. Sometimes there is canned fruit, canned without sugar, kept packed down in cottonseed to prevent its freezing, and eaten only when "granulated sweetenin' " (sugar) is available. "Long sweetenin' (molasses) ain't no 'count fer fruit."

Occasionally string beans or corn or tomatoes are "put up." Many families make no attempt to preserve these vegetables for winter use. For those who do, they may ferment for lack of proper canning methods or equipment. "I put up some tomatoes but they all sp'iled. I reckon it was 'cause my rings or tops, one, was old."

Perishable vegetables do not keep well in a country where one day may be cold and raw, and the next day may be bright and warm. Irish potatoes and yams and cabbages can be kept for awhile, if the weather is not too warm and there is an abundance of straw or cottonseed to pack them in to prevent their freezing. Often the potato crop fails and there are none to keep.

There is generally no desire for, and often an aversion to, vegetables or fruits out of season. Carrots given out by the Government relief commissary have been found in ditches along the roadside, for it was not natural and therefore did not seem quite right to some of the people, to have carrots in midwinter. Oranges, on the other hand, are prized novelties. There are no preconceived notions about them. They are shared with friends, and those who get none are envious.

Usually a family has corn meal, but sometimes even that is scarce. "We had two more bushels of corn to be ground, but it got nits in it and warn't fitten fer bread, so we're a-feedin' it to the chickens."

The normal winter diet of the average mountain family consists of dried beans and black-eyed peas, smoked salt meat, corn bread (corn pone), and some light bread (made of wheat flour), sorghum molasses, coffee, and sometimes canned fruit.

Lacking good yeast, lean meat, milk, eggs, and fresh vegetables, the people have "plagery" and rickets, and they do not know why.

"Housekeeping Aides" are now being sent in to some hill sections to try to show the importance of food variation and the science of a balanced diet. What a pioneering spirit such an "aide" must have in order to teach these people! Imagine a woman with a modern education in dietetics, trying to illustrate to a mountain woman the intricacies of a balanced menu, when all the material she finds at hand to work with is salt pork, flour, corn meal, beans, sorghum, baking powder, soda, salt, and perhaps a can of unsweetened wild blackberries, and some eggs and milk. The mountain woman would probably have to show the expert how to cook over an open fire or on a wood-heated stove, with only one or two pots at her disposal.

The housekeeping teacher finds no commercially canned foods. There are no can-opening experts among the mountain women. A pile of empty cans in a yard would mean that the people who use that yard came from out of the hills.

At first she has to confine herself to teaching the women to cook well the things for which they have the ingredients; to make bread a little less "sad," and to swim the beans in a little less greasy water.

The Brogdons' winter schedule is quite different from that of the summer.

On a bright day John and the boys may do repair jobs on the place—patch a leak in the roof or mend some harness. They may clear a field or cut firewood. If spring is near they may take the plow in the wagon to the home of an aged or ailing neighbor, and plow his garden plot for him. And the grateful neighbor will exclaim, "You-uns be mighty good to us old things, and the Lord'll bless you fer it!"

Sarah and the girls will wash, or clean the house, or make clothing for the family, explaining, "We're all jest plumb naked fer clothes!" In the afternoon they may do some fancywork—embroidery on unbleached muslin, crocheting or knitting or rug weaving. They may invite some neighbor women in for a quilting or a sewing bee.

Even if they can read they probably will not. Reading matter is scarce, and the scope of their information and interest is narrowly limited.

The whole family may go to a butchering or house raising, to a nut gathering or molasses making, or other "workin's."

In the evening they may all go to an entertainment given by the school children, to a church "sociable," or to a box or a pie supper.

These suppers are given at schools or churches in order to raise money. Each girl or woman who attends brings a pie or a box of food, made as attractive as she can make it. Great secrecy accompanies the smuggling in of the boxes, as no one is supposed to know who brings any one of them. Each one is auctioned off. The men do the bidding. After all have been sold, each successful bidder enjoys his newly acquired sustenance in the company of its creator, and the proceeds of the sale are appropriated to some worthy cause, possibly to a fund for a map for the school or for hymnals for the church.

The family may all go to a dance, held at a home or in a barn or school building.

School or barn dances are public. A home dance is supposedly private. Word is whispered around, "Martins is givin' a dance up to their place tonight. They want that you-all should come. But if anyone asts you about it disremember you've heerd tell of it. If them Hicks boys gits wind of it there'll be trouble."

Each neighborhood seems to have a few young men who delight in getting news of a private dance or party, attending unasked, and disturbing the invited guests. The boys may not have been invited because they have won for themselves a reputation for rowdyism, or because their families do not measure up to local social standards. Perhaps they are considered low class, or "suggins," or perhaps they are newcomers—which might simply mean that their grandparents did not live in the neighborhood.

These same boys may be the ringleaders of brawls at public dances. Many of the young men seek to heighten their enjoyment of such an occasion by imbibing strong mountain liquor. As the evening wears on, tempers grow short. A bullying braggart may easily start a fracas. The dance is likely to end, for a number of them, with a fight—with fists, knives, or guns. The "best people" leave "before a fraction starts." By the next day, when the men are all sober, enmities of the evening before seem to be forgotten, and the neighborhood goes calmly and peacefully on its way.

A stormy winter day is not so full of activity and sociability. The family sleeps a little later than usual. The animals are cared for, and during the rest of the day, except at mealtimes, the members of the family sit by the fire and talk or doze. They may shell nuts, roast apples, or pop corn. The light will be insufficient for close work if the doors must be kept closed.

Sunday is another day for sociability. If there is to be a preacher in the neighborhood the people will prepare their basket dinners and go to church.

If there is no church service one family will spend the day with another. During the afternoon the women will stay at the house and discuss their interests—sewing, cooking, child care, housekeeping, and their neighbors. The men will saunter out to the barn lot to appraise the stock, and discuss animal care, farming, prices, politics, religion, and their neighbors.

The father of a family is often unable to tell the ages of the children or the state of the family clothing or the quantity or variety of food on hand. But the mother cannot tell how long a sack of flour lasts or what it costs, or how many pounds of cotton the family raised last year, or how much they were paid for it, for the man does all the tradin'. And she is not likely to know the number of acres in the farm or the number that they have cultivated. Both parents probably know exactly how many mules and cows and pigs they own, but the man needs to ask his wife how many chickens she has.

The whole family knows about the young stock. If the cow "has jest drapped a calf," or the horse has foaled or there is a new litter of pigs, that is big news to be shared with all comers. So also is the death of a cow or a mule.

On a Sunday afternoon the girls will stroll down the road or through the woods or sit in a comfortable tree, and talk.

The boys may strike out for the nearest settlement or crossroads store.

A typical mountain hamlet may have two or three stores. These are general stores, stocked with a great variety of goods—clothing, hardware, groceries, furniture and household furnishings, and other miscellany. Such stores are a boon to jobbers who are there able to unload merchandise that has long been out of favor elsewhere. Here the turnover of stock is slow, the display is seldom rearranged or dusted, and an item is not reordered until the supply on hand is exhausted.

Brooms, or work gloves, are hung in bunches from the ceiling; tin cups or eggs are piled up in wire wastebaskets. Customers must not be finicky about modern sanitary packaging. Pickles are dipped out of barrels, sugar is sold from an opened

In a crossroads store

Going visiting

sack, combs and whistles are tried out by any curious loafer.

In one corner of one of these stores is the post office, "kept" by the owner of the store. He has abundant time to study all mail that comes in, read periodicals and postcards, and brood over postmarks, if he is a sociable man, interested in his neighbors.

In addition to the stores there will be a garage and filling station, a blacksmith shop, a school, a church, and a few houses. There may also be a gristmill and a cotton gin.

When the boys get to town they will spend the afternoon sitting on a store porch, if the weather is fine, or gathered around the stove inside, if it is cold.

On the way to and from the store they will amuse themselves by throwing rocks or shooting. Road signs and billboards are favorite targets. If a window is hit, it probably will not be the first time it has been hit.

Christmas is celebrated in the good old Southern way with firecrackers if they can be had, or, lacking these, with the ever available rifle gun or shotgun. Other holidays receive less notice. Winter is largely made up of holidays. Summer is work time. But remember that the farming season runs from February or March to November or December.

12

Health Problems

For want of a nail, the shoe was lost,
For want of the shoe, the horse was lost,
For want of the horse, the rider was lost,
For want of the rider, the battle was lost,
For want of the battle, the kingdom was lost,
And all for the want of a horse-shoe nail.

"SARIE!" JOHN BROGDON CALLED TO HIS WIFE. HE was returning from his morning trip to the mailbox, his usually deliberate gait touched with just a suggestion of hurry. "Sarie, Charlie, he brung the mail this mornin'. He's ben a-tellin' me as how Gran'maw Taylor is took plumb bad with a risin' on her leg. Ted 'lows as how he reckons she's like to die."

"Land sakes!" Sarah exclaimed as she put her flatiron back on the hearth near the coals and came out onto the porch. "Is Maw sick? She was ailin' last time I was over to Addie's but she warn't down bad. We better go."

"Yeah, 'spect we had. George, you call the team and hitch up the wagon. Put in some feed fer 'em. Jack, your maw and me and the rest'll go and you stay here and look after the place.

"Aw, Paw. I want to go to see Gran'maw, too."

"Sorry, son, but you're the biggest. We'll tell your gran'maw you hankered to go."

"I'll be right proud if you will."

"Bert, you run fetch a nice middlin' from the smokehouse, and Margetta, you git a jar of them peaches out'n the storm cellar and see if you kin find some eggs, and then come change your duds." Mrs. Brogdon was already dressing the younger children.

When George drove the wagon around the house Mr. Brogdon threw in a sack of black-eyed peas with the other things to be taken to the Justices, and Mrs. Brogdon sent a "poke of cold victuals" for a lunch on the way. One by one as they were ready, the children came out and climbed into the wagon. The spring seat was saved for Sarah and the "least one," the two-year-old Joey, and Bud, who was "sort of ailin' " this day. John climbed in last and stood up in the wagon bed behind them, to drive.

It was four or five miles to the home of Ted and Addie Justice. "Hit'll be mighty rough, so you kids hang on," John warned. "Some of the way there ain't hardly no road, you might say. But it'll be right smart better'n walkin'."

No able seaman on a storm-tossed deck has need of worthier sea legs than had he as the wagon went rocking and bumping and careening over boulders and around trees, up and down hill. Occasionally there was no sign of a road, and he picked his own way. A car could never have followed the same course. But it was indeed "a heap sight better'n walkin'."

As they bumped along, the Brogdons worried about Mrs. Brogdon's kinfolk.

"Maw an' Paw hadn't rightly orter be with Ted

and Addie. They was havin' a hard enough time exportin' their own selves. Ted, he's a good boy [any man is a boy to those who know his parents] and mighty kindhearted, but he don't never seem to git ahead none. By rights there hain't no sunning-law orter keep 'em. But what kin they do when they ain't got no boys. And to think that Maw had thirteen! But they's only three left, and them's all girls."

John broke in, "Gran'paw, he worked as long as he was financially able, but sence he got porely they's ben nothin' fer it but fer first one and another of the folks to help 'em. I'd jest as lief have 'em with us fer another spell, but Ted figgers we got ten kids and him and Addie ain't got but four, so they kin take 'em better'n we kin."

"By rights Jim and Fannie had orter keep 'em."

"I'd be powerful sorry fer the old folks. Jim kin git mighty ugly if he's crossed. He's jest plain ornery," John threw in.

Sarah ignored the interruption. "They're the best fixed of any of us. But he's close, and she is, too. They allers have some reason to give why they cain't help out." One wheel of the wagon dropped off a rock as she finished and made the "out" an ejaculation. The listening children giggled.

Sarah looked around to make sure the family and the food had not bounced off. "Watch them eggs," she warned.

"Oh, shuckins, Maw!" Margetta exclaimed. "I taken the peaches and plumb forgot to git the eggs."

"There ain't nothin' fer it now but to go on,"

Sarah decided. "Chances are Jim and Fannie won't bring *nothin'* if they come."

When the sun was overhead they stopped under the trees by a cold, clear spring to "eat a snack," although they had not much farther to go. "They won't be set fer a bunch like this to run in on 'em jest at mealtime," Sarah explained.

They reached the home of the Justices in the early afternoon. It was a house of the old type. There was a gallery across the front. The only doors of the two rooms faced each other across the open passage.

"Hain't no one else come yit. The Lord bless Charlie fer makin' mention of it to us!" exclaimed Sarah, seeing no other vehicles by the house.

A boy came to open the gate. John skillfully maneuvered the wagon between a crosscut saw lying near a pile of red cedar posts Ted had been cutting, and an old sow feeding a litter of pigs. The mother pig seemed entirely unconcerned by the wagon until it got too uncomfortably close to her family. Then they all ran away, grunting and squealing shrilly, ears flopping and tails bouncing.

"I shore am proud to see you all," Addie greeted them. "Light down and come on in. Maw'll be right pleased. She's took purty bad."

They mounted the porch by means of two stumps of different lengths, which served as steps, and entered the room to the left of the passage.

Old Grandma Taylor was lying in one of the double beds. Her face was drawn with suffering. Her "How be ye?" was weak.

Grandpa Taylor was sitting by the one window,

a big family Bible open on his knee. His spectacles, which were in all probability only magnifying glasses brought to him from the ten-cent store, lacked one lens and one bow. That side was held up by a rubber band slipped over his ear. He was apparently absorbed in his reading and did not glance up.

Addie nodded in his direction. "He don't hear us. Ever sence Maw took to the bed he jest sets there, a-mullin' over that there Bible."

"What's ailin' you, Maw?" Sarah enquired.

"Hit's my laig," her mother answered slowly. "I had a sore on it and perfection [infection] set up and it riz. Hit's a-runnin' now, so I reckon the pizen's a-comin' out."

Painfully she raised herself onto one elbow and reached to pull back the covers. John and Ted, guessing what was coming, left the room and seated themselves on the passage floor just outside the open door, their backs against the wall.

Grandma Taylor pulled away the covers to expose a black cotton stocking. "I'm a-keepin' of it on to keep from dirtyin' the quilts," she explained.

When, with Addie's help, she rolled the stocking down they saw a badly swollen leg with ugly dark streaks shooting out from a festering sore. "I politiced it with hog lard, but it didn't do it no good so I decided I'd try a-payin' it no mind and see if it wouldn't heal its own self."

"Hit's wearisome fer Maw a-layin' down," Addie said. "She cain't lay on her right side, fer that's the sore one, and of course she hain't ben able to lay on her left side fer many a year, 'count of

her heart drippin' if she does, so she's got to lay
flat of her back."

The old man by the window broke in, "How be
ye, Sarie?"

"Tolerable, Paw. How're you?"

He saw that she spoke but he didn't understand.
"Heh?" he asked, cupping his hand behind his ear.
She repeated her question more loudly. Still he
didn't comprehend. Addie, more accustomed to
making him hear, came to her rescue and shouted
her question to him. He understood then, answered
politely, "Right porely, thank 'e," and went back to
his reading.

Addie explained, "We've all ben a-gruntin'
around with colds, and them rheumatiz is catchin'
holt of him agin."

"I hear Jim and Fannie a-comin'. I'd know the
noise of Jim's car anywheres," Ted called.

One of the boys ran to open the gate, and the
car drew up near the house.

Jim and Fannie Combs and the baby and three
children got out. Sarah looked significantly at
John—a silent "I told you so!" Jim and Fannie had
brought no provisions.

Soon the women were seated in the room with
Grandma Taylor again. After she had repeated
the painful procedure of showing her leg to Fannie,
the men came in too.

The adults seated themselves on the other bed,
or on the low "split-bottom" chairs drawn up in
front of the fireplace, where a black pot of beans
and salt pork was simmering in the coals.

There were children everywhere, seated on the

hearth, standing in the doorway, running through the passage and shouting in the yard. They went in and out of the room, staying if the conversation interested them and leaving when it did not. Occasionally one of the larger boys would bring in a log for the fire.

Quiet or privacy for illness is almost impossible to arrange in a mountain home. The bed is ordinarily in the room where the family lives, and the family life goes right on around the invalid.

Fannie broke a moment of silence. "Well, it jest goes to show that I was right! Goin' on two year ago Doc Marshall told Maw she had ort to have an operation right then, fer cancer. I says to her, 'Good land, Maw,' I says, 'don't do nothin' like that. Never let no doctor go a-cuttin' on you. You go right out and see old Aunt Liza Turner, out to Mountain Gap. She kin brew you some roots and herbs what'll fix you up right now. She's got secrets don't nobody else know,' I says. Maw, she'd ben flat of her back fer three months, but I'd have you know that no sooner than she'd got some of Aunt Liza's stuff in her than she begin to pick up. You-all know it's the truth. And now, seems like, she's a-goin' to die of somethin' else."

Grandma moaned softly.

"Hesh up, Fannie. What sort of a way is that to be a-talkin', and Maw still here?" Addie warned.

"I don't take no stock of doctors nohow," Fannie justified herself. "Aunt Liza Turner, she was a-takin' care of folks hereabouts long afore Doc Marshall was borned."

"I think Doc knows more'n Mis' Turner," Sarah

disagreed. "He give my kids shots fer smallpox, and when the Smiths, next down from us, had 'em, none of mine taken 'em. I consist on shots fer my kids jest as soon as they're big enough."

"Maybe they wouldn't of took 'em nohow. You cain't say fer sartin," Jim interposed reasonably.

"Hain't no doc goin' to stick no needles in my kids!" Fannie was emphatic. "I've heerd tell of 'em dyin' of it."

"That county agent come wantin' to stick a needle in my cows a week sence, come Saturday," Jim guffawed. "The young fool!"

"I sorter figger about both man and beast, that they'll live till their time comes and then they'll die, no difference what you do. 'The Lord giveth, and the Lord taketh away.' " Ted ventured.

The old woman on the bed seemed to be asleep.

"Earl, he told me about goin' over on the ferry-boat jest after the last overflow," Ted continued. "There was some strange folks a-crossin', too. His kids ast fer a drink, and he done jest like he allers does—he got a old can out'n his wagon and given 'em all some water. The furrin lady told him he hadn't orter a-done it. Looks like she'd a ben thirsty, too. The sight of water does that to most anyone. Some folks do git plumb quar notions."

"I wish I knowed the straight of this here malaria talk," Addie said. "I'd allers heerd it was the night air what give it to you, and Lutie Magness says it comes from skeeter bites. How's a body to know?"

"I hold to the night air 'er swamp vapors, I don't rightly know which," Fannie declared. "But I don't reckon it makes you no difference where it comes from. As long as you keep the doors closed at night and take quinine you cain't do no more no-how."

"John, he ain't had his yit this year," Sarah bragged, and they all looked at John as though he were a wonder.

Fannie drew the attention back to herself. "I shore had a skeer last week. I heerd Little Jim a-hollerin' fit ter kill and I run out to see what ailed him. He'd fell and cut his wrist on a old piece of glass in the yard and the blood was a-spurtin' out. I grabbed him up and run in to the chimney fer a handful of soot, and plastered it on the cut place and covered it good with sugar and tied it on with a rag. Hit stopped in no time, but I was weak as a cat and a-shakin' all over."

Suppose Fannie had been out of sugar when Little Jim cut his wrist. Of course she might have used cobwebs.

And who could blame her? She was doing the best thing she knew. The fact that her method was the remnant of theory two hundred years old, only confirmed her in her faith in it. Her ancestors had brought the medical lore of the eighteenth century into the hills. Leaving apothecaries behind, they had substituted herbs and plants found in their new environment, for their former medicines. They had brought some superstitions and, as part of the old knowledge slipped out of mind, had added new superstitions to replace it. A chance act, happening to precede a desired result, might thereafter be considered the cause of that result. When

To market, to market

Closed to keep out the night air

An old stone well

Table rocks

such a premise had won general acceptance, even the skeptic who might privately question the relation of cause and effect, would feel it safer to conform to the approved way, as long as a surer one was lacking. It might propitiate whatever Fate requires that we do what we can.

So a set of healing methods was built up, partly based on fact, as in the case of some herbs which, by happy chance, were really found to be of benefit for certain ailments; and partly on mere superstitions, which were entirely worthless, except as an implicit faith in their efficacy gave them psychological therapeutic power.

Medical enlightenment increased all around the mountains, but little of it got in to them. Patent-medicine vendors pushed in and found a ready market, for cure-alls were not new to these people. Their local treatments were often similarly diversely useful. It is a mystery now where the money comes from out of these hills, for the quantities of nostrums which are bought as panaceas, with implicit faith from drugstores in town, from the crossroad store, or from the peddler's wagon.

But there has been no commercial interest to carry more authentic medical information to the mountaineers. And there has been scant opportunity for them to secure it.

There are no women's clubs studying new developments in treatment of disease; they do not hear health lectures on the radio nor read of the latest medical discoveries in books or magazines or newspapers. Facts of sanitation, control of communicable disease, modern medicine and surgery, which are the common possession of the man in the street, are still only heresay, some considered silly and some terrifying, to the man and the woman of the hills.

Sarah had been pondering over Fannie's story. "I think when a body's hurt it's better to git to the doctor," she affirmed. "I don't set no store by them old ways."

"Pshaw, child," her mother roused up. "Your great-gran'maw was one of the best blood stoppers and charm brewers this valley ever seed. I recollect one time——" Her voice trailed off and she dozed again. It made no difference. They all knew the story well.

Addie took up the conversation. "They say old man Cummin's's woman kin stop blood. I've never seed her do it, but Neva was a-tellin' me. She says t'other day the Wider Hall's least one made a mislick with a choppin'-ax and cut his foot nigh off. In spite of all she could do she couldn't stop the bleedin' so she taken and packed him on her back over to old man Cummin's's. She set him down, still bleedin', on a chair and old lady Cummin's made some signs with her hands over his foot and kinda sung out some words so low couldn't none of 'em understand 'em, like she was talkin' to someone clost what they-uns couldn't see, and, 'I'm tellin' you the truth,' Neva says, 'the bleedin' quit right now, jest like it had ben shet off,' she says. She's seed her do it with her own eyes. I don't know, myself."

This story seemed a climax. No one could think of an appropriate one to follow it just then, and the conversation shifted to other matters as the afternoon wore on. Finally Addie rose.

"The sun's gittin' down. I reckon I better fix some victuals." She went out to the room across the hallway, and Sarah followed her. The men went out to see about the evening chores. Grandpa slept in his chair, snoring softly.

When the evening meal was ready the men and older boys were called first. The crowd was much too large all to be seated at the table at the same time. They took the chairs from the fireplace and supplemented this seating with a box, a lard can, and a flour barrel. When the men had finished their meal Addie washed their plates and forks in the dishpan on the stove, and the women were served. They, too, had some of the beans and salt pork that had been simmering by the fire all day, and corn bread that had been cooked in an uncovered skillet on top of the stove. The children stood by the table to eat until their plates of beans were empty, and then took their hunks of corn bread outdoors with them as they went back to their play.

There were flies on the table. No one mentioned the undesirability of letting them in the house and on the food. If anyone had done so, Addie's astonished response would have been, "But what kin you do about flies? Don't everybody have 'em?" Any suggestion of screens would have come as an entirely new and unique idea. She didn't know anybody who had screens. And if there were screens wouldn't the flies come through the cracks between the logs where the dobbing was out? But Ted couldn't afford screens anyway and neither could the rest of them, so why raise such a question?

By the time the dishes were washed again and the crumbs brushed away, night had fallen. One by one the women left the house and went into the woods in one direction and, by some prearrangement, the men disappeared in the other. There had been a toilet on the place when the house was new but it had fallen down long ago, and Ted had never got around to building another.

All sat by the fire, without other light, until the children were nodding. Then Addie lighted a lamp for each room, and the household made ready for the night. Addie and Ted and their family slept in the room with the old folks, as usual, except that, because of Grandma's discomfort, only Grandpa slept with her this night and the extra child joined the others on the pallet on the floor. The women visitors and their children were made as comfortable as possible on pallets in the other room, and the men and older boys rolled up in quilts on the gallery or in the yard. Soon all was quiet except for the patter of rats scampering over the floor. Twice during the night Addie got up to try to ease Grandma's pain.

The next morning, just as the dishes were done, Jess and Mary Bales, who lived on the next fork upstream, arrived with some of their family, to see how Grandma was feeling.

"We gotta be back by chore time," Jess Bales announced. "Some of the kids is at school and will be home then."

Mrs. Bales indicated a boy of about twelve. "This

young-un here has ben down sick. He had diphthery
last week and he ain't right peart yit. And the girl
here was puny today so we jest kept 'em home from
school."

Grandma was weaker than the day before and
did not offer to show her leg to Mary Bales.
Mary sought to combine comfort and advice. "I
had a sore on my limb a while back. I'd ben a-work-
in' in the yard and I didn't know fer sartin what
ailed it but I knowed it was a snake bite or a spider
bite or a bruise, one. I tried a-puttin' turpentine
on it first off, a-thinkin' it might be a spider bite,
but the center didn't drop out so I know'd it warn't
that. I drug around with it fer a spell. The misery
begun to run up my limb, and it went higher and
higher till it was clean to my back and I was nigher
dead nor alive. Then I recollected what the Bible
says to do and I done it. I soaked a rag in coal oil
and I wropped it around. And every time it dried
out I dipped it agin and wropped it around, fer the
Good Book says, 'Nothin' but the oil of the earth
will cure you in the latter days.' And first thing I
knowed it was cured. See!" and she showed where
her bruise had been.

Before long another visitor arrived. She had
walked from her home two miles up the valley carrying a year-old baby astraddle of her hip. The
mother was Dolly Reeves. She must have been a
cunning baby to have been named "Dolly." She had
outlived the appropriateness of the designation.

"Bill, he 'lowed he'd like to come along but he
warn't fitten," she apologized for her husband. "I
don't know what ails him. He's ben puny fer quite

a spell now, and fer goin' on two weeks he's run a
fever. Hit may be flu or it may be typhoid. We
cain't afford a doctor nor no 'scription so I ben
a-givin' him some quinine and some pills I had in
the house. I don't know what kind of pills they be
or what they be fer, but I reckoned I'd try 'em as
long as they was right there and was all I had."

"I got some medicine here I was give fer fever
oncet. I set a powerful store by it. I'll give you
some to take to Bill when you go. You make mention of it if I forgit," Addie offered.

"Thank 'e kindly," Mary was pleased and grateful. Medicine takes cash money. "Hain't it quar
how everything hits you at once, seems like? I'd
have you know, every last one of my bunch has
measles, 'ceptin' me and Bill and the little-un. I
couldn't git 'em 'cause I'm a-nursin' her."

On this theory how little opportunity most mountain mothers would have to "ketch" anything!

"Where'd they git 'em?" Addie was concerned
for her younger children.

"From the Clarks' kids, yon side of us. They
come played with my kids in our wood lot after
they was broke out. I ast Mattie why she let 'em
come, and she said if I didn't want my kids to git
what her bunch has I'd ort of kept 'em away from
hern."

There is no attempt at quarantine in the hills.
Children who have a disease, or who have been
exposed and therefore have no fear of further exposure, continue to circulate freely in society.

The principle of putting the responsibility on the
parents of well children, to keep them away from

sick ones, if they do not wish them to be exposed to a communicable disease, is generally accepted. If the same lack of care for exposure existed when these parents were children, it seems unaccountable that, so often now, the parents contract measles or mumps or the other children's diseases when their children do. Why didn't they have them in their own childhood? Perhaps these are return engagements. But it is no unusual thing to find all of a family down at the same time, with no one able to care for the others, so that a neighbor or relative must be called in to nurse, if one can be got.

Regardless of the disease, children are allowed to run and play as long as they feel like it, and go to bed only when it suits them. Complications, often far worse than the original malady, frequently result.

So much of the illness is absolutely unnecessary —the result of ignorance or of want. One wonders how people manage to live under such conditions. Many of them don't manage. Many children die in infancy. Those strong enough to survive in spite of the lack of sanitation, the faulty diet, the epidemics, and home remedies, live. But the results of the strain to which their systems have been subjected in sustaining life become evident as they grow older. Many more persons are "ailin' " or "puny" or "jest gruntin' around" than are perfectly strong and well, and few live to be old.

"Hit goes easier with 'em to have 'em while they're young anyhow," Fannie consoled Mary.

With this beginning for the morning's visiting they were well started on another discussion of illness and death. Bedside conversation always seems to turn irresistibly that way.

For awhile they exchanged news.

"Did you hear about Tom Jenkins?" Sarah didn't look directly at Fannie, but her aim was accurate. "He had Doc Jones cut his appendix out."

"Well, if he ain't a blowed-up sucker!" Fannie exclaimed. "I told Mis' Jenkins that if she'd git a tube of [she mentioned a patent medicine] and rub it on the knot on his side, it would go away." And the debate of doctor versus home treatment was on.

"He tried that and he was out of the bed fer a spell," Sarah admitted. "But he taken another attack last Monday and was all doubled up in knots."

Just then two of the little children, playing tag, raced into the room, and one of them, in his effort to elude the other, scrambled across the foot of his grandmother's bed. His mother seized him and ran him out of the room, paddling as she went, but the damage was already done. Grandma Taylor groaned and then wept, whimpering softly. Ted moved over and sat in the doorway, blocking it. At last, soothed by Sarah, Grandma dozed again, and John took up the story where it had been interrupted.

"Tom, he's on Earl Magness's place, and last year he didn't hardly make more'n enough to pay taxes, fer havin' them spells. So when Earl heerd about this one he went and told Tom he'd have to find someplace else, and leave him git another bunch in what could do better. Tom, he begged to stay and promised he'd git a operation right off. So he did."

"And now he's to git to stay," Sarah finished triumphantly.

There is not much place for the chronic invalid in the hills unless he owns his own land and can rent it, or has grown sons to care for him. A landowner wants a family of the best physique he can find to tend his place.

When the news was all told they turned to a rediscussion of things they all knew.

They bemoaned the fact that Ted "was down sick from August to December," so the Justices had lost most of their corn, because the children were too young to gather it properly at the right time.

Fannie reported, "Jim, he's got vericle veins from a-hikin' in the army and he ain't got no pension in a right smart while now."

She also told, at length, about one of their neighbors who "went down sudden three year ago and hain't ben fitten fer work sence, and he couldn't doctor 'cause they couldn't afford the 'scriptions. And then when the crops was in, the boy laid down and had convulsions and the cows jumped up and got sick, and the whole business that fall cost 'em twenty dollars."

What an important part illness plays in the lives of these people! Economically they are perpetually so close pressed that there is no slack for emergencies. In case of serious illness, followed by death, it is often true that "hit taken all they'd laid by to keep 'em fer the winter to doctor her and to

put her away." Very little of this may have gone
to the doctor for his doctoring. Most of it may have
gone to feed guests, for it is customary for all the
relatives who can leave their own places to come to
the home of the sick one, bringing all the younger
children along. It may develop into a family re-
union. They come ostensibly to help—or to mourn,
if the outcome is what they expect. Actually they
often succeed only in adding to the crowding and
confusion of the limited quarters, in convincing the
patient that he must indeed be ill enough to die, and
in multiplying the number to be fed by someone
whose time may be needed for nursing.

If the illness is not so serious, and comes at a
convenient time of year, the family may be little
affected economically, for there are no wages lost,
and there are no doctor bills in cases of common
ailments for which some more experienced neighbor always knows the remedy. But if it comes at
a crucial time, when the efforts of the family are
needed for the crop, it may be disastrous. "We
couldn't plant no crop last spring fer we was all
laid up with the scarlet fever at plantin' time,"
may mean the difference between independence and
dependence.

They talked about their "cute innerjession."
Here appendicitis may still be acute indigestion,
and mastoditis or delirium tremens may be brain
fever. They talked about "very close veins," about
Dolly's boy's "spinal attic," which was incurable,
and about Sarah's operation for "white swelling."
And again, as the women approached the more inti-
mate details of their family's physical ills, the men,

knowing what was coming, tactfully slipped out of the room.

Dolly took her baby and the fever medicine, and left before the noon meal was served, but the Bales stayed till midafternoon.

Grandma was very restless. Her sleep was fitful. Though she complained very little and seemed drowsy, she was obviously suffering. As soon as the Bales had gone, the rest, as though drawn by their common concern, met under the big tree in the yard, for a "confab." The children, seeming to sense the seriousness of the situation, withdrew to the other side of the house.

"I think we'd orter send fer Doc Marshall," Addie declared herself. "I'm scairt about Maw. Seems like she's recked with pain."

"How about sendin' fer Aunt Liza?" Fannie suggested, but her tone lacked conviction.

"You know Aunt Liza's too old to come," Jim spoke sharply.

"This ain't no time fer triflin'," Sarah looked determined. "Maw's bad off, and I think we better git Doc Marshall here as quick as ever we kin."

"I'll go to Givens's store and call him on the telephone," John offered.

"Hit'll be dark afore you could git there," Ted warned.

"That don't make me no difference," John assured them.

Fannie motioned to Jim, and they withdrew from the crowd. When they rejoined the others Fannie announced, "Jim'll take you in his car, John. You should git back afore dark that-a-way."

Even Fannie and Jim now recognized that they all faced a crisis serious enough to warrant the putting aside of pettiness.

"Who'll tell Paw?" Addie asked, troubled. It was agreed that Sarah should, and she went to get him. Hers was a difficult task. Sending for a doctor was an open admission that they feared for their mother's life, and their father would know it.

In the mountains a doctor is called only as a last resort. In common with that great number of their fellow citizens in this country, who have too much to receive or accept free medical care and too little to be able to pay for it except in serious and evident emergency, doctors are a luxury. The situation must be extremely acute to justify calling one, for the customary home visiting fee of a dollar a mile, is more than the average mountain family can readily pay.

This charge is not exorbitant from the doctor's standpoint. A trip into the hills is more expensive than one on a highway not only because running a car in second or low gear increases the consumption of gas and oil, but also because twisting and bumping a car over rough mountain roads causes much greater wear on brakes, tires, and frame. Some doctors will drive to the nearest point on a highway and have the family meet them there with a wagon.

And a trip of this sort takes much time. Many patients could be visited in town during the same number of hours. A doctor with a family to support cannot afford to make country trips too readily or he will find his time filled by a poorly paying mountain practice.

Most of the town doctors do some charity work in the hills. And often, fitting the bill to the financial status, they care for patients unable to pay the standard charge—patients who call them only when the need is real, and who are conscientious in their efforts at remuneration.

Some families will call a doctor on slight provocation, at any hour of the day or night, without thought of paying him. They will change doctors frequently, and sometimes have to produce a little money to persuade one to come. But most families expect to pay their doctor bill, consider it a moral obligation, and worry over it, although they may pay their loan from the bank or the general store first, in order to save the mule or the cow they have put up as collateral.

"My girl has had a pain in her side fer goin' on three days now. I hain't sent fer the doctor cause we hain't paid him fer the last two trips and I jest hate to, though he said we was to go ahead and let him know if any of us got up in the bed sick," is an expression of a common sentiment.

Anxious to clear itself of debt, and despairing of accumulating enough cash to meet the bill, a family may take eggs or chickens or hams or potatoes to the doctor. A doctor's wife is kept busy during the fruit season, canning the fruit brought in by the patients. Perhaps a mountain woman will do quilting for her, or come into town once a week to do her laundry work or cleaning, if she lives close enough to town and has some means of transportation. A doctor receives his pay in all sorts of benefits. Sometimes he wishes for more of the compensation in currency with which he might pay his own bills.

Occasionally a bill is paid in cash, but a little at a time—fifteen cents for a dozen eggs sold in town, seventy-five cents for a load of wood delivered. It takes a long time to pay a fifty-dollar bill this way, and other illness may come frequently enough to keep the family always in debt to the doctor.

It was after dark when John and Jim returned.

"We like to never got Doc Marshall," Jim reported. "Two trees what Givens had his wire strung on blowed down two weeks back and broke the wire, and he ain't got it fixed yit. He told us about a feller about ten mile yon side of him, what had a phone. I disremember his name. So we went on there. His line was strung along a fence fer a ways and it was hard to hear, fer the wind was a-bangin' the wire agin the fence. I could hear it sparkin' when it hit."

"Behories, I thought he'd never make Doc hear," Jim chuckled. "He yelled till he should of heerd him withouten no phone."

"When's he comin'?" Addie was in no mood for levity.

"First thing in the mornin'."

"Bless you fer takin' John, Jim," Sarah said. "Lord knows when he'd of got back on old Bess."

Grandma's three daughters took turns sitting up with the patient that night. They had decided to try poultices on her leg again. The wind that had bothered Jim's telephone call had got steadily stronger and colder so that the fire needed frequent tending. The men and boys, who had slept the night before in the yard or on the gallery, huddled together in the passage. For a long time Grandma's moans accompanied the moaning wind. A hound howled near the house. None but the little children got much sleep.

When morning came the wind still blew, cold and penetrating, and a miserably raw drizzle was falling. In order to protect her mother from draughts Addie had fastened a quilt over the window and hung another over the door, in such a way that it had to be raised and pulled aside before the door could be opened. The sickroom was lighted by the fire and an oil lamp on a stand.

Grandma Taylor could have been made more comfortable in a hospital, but she would never have consented to go to one. There are few hospitals in the hills. Hospitalization entails leaving familiar, trusted things for strange, frightening ones. Those few people who allow themselves to be taken, usually do so only when all else has failed. Consequently, the percentage of those who do not return home alive is high. Therefore, to the mountaineer, going to a hospital has come to be almost synonymous with going away from home to die, and most of them are unwilling to risk it.

Doctor Marshall came early. Only the women and Grandpa stayed in the room while he examined Grandma. The others all gathered in the room across the passage. He finished his examination quickly and gave Grandma a hypodermic injection, to Fannie's keen distress.

"No use to let her suffer like this," he answered her objection.

Then he went out and called John out of the other room and they walked to the gallery together.

The women came out to the passage, and Grandpa came shuffling out after them.

"Sarie," he asked in the dull, low monotone of the very deaf, "What's he say? Hit's mighty hard to jest set and watch y'all a-talkin', a-wantin' to know so bad what ye say, and not be able to git no notion of it." The old man's eyes filled with tears.

Sarah put a strong, kind arm around him, and together they went to join John and the doctor on the gallery. Soon they all knew the verdict. The children were sent to the barn to play.

The doctor, Grandpa, and the three daughters, stayed with Grandma during the day. The rest only looked in occasionally.

By noon the wind and the rain had stopped and the sun shone bright and warm. Addie removed the quilts from the window and door, for the air in the room was foul and heavy with the odor of medicines. The children went to the hill pasture far from the house.

In the late afternoon Doctor Marshall came out of the sickroom with his hat and bag. "All over," he announced, and left.

Addie came out. "She's gone," she sobbed.

Sarah followed her, wiping her own eyes, as she sought to comfort her sister. "Her sufferin's over. We kin praise the Lord fer that. I'm proud we got Doc here to ease her at the last."

"Paw, he's goin' to be powerful lost. He's jest

An Ozark stream

A graveyard on a hilltop

a-settin' there a-holdin' her hand and a-lookin' at her," Addie wept on Sarah's comforting shoulder. "He had her longer'n most. Maw was fifty-six." Fannie's eyes were damp, but, the crisis over, she was rapidly returning to normal.

"She shore was a mighty good woman, and Addie's like her," Ted affirmed.

The unexpectedness of this commendation from her husband served to stop Addie's sobs. Mountain men are not given to compliments.

Just then the children, who had seen the doctor drive away, began to arrive quietly at the house, and all eyes were wiped. The children must not see their parents crying.

Death was not new to any but the younger children. They tiptoed softly into the room where their grandmother lay, to stare in awed silence at her still form and touch her cheek with a questioning, gentle finger. Only the very small ones tried to talk with her.

Doctor Marshall had probably mentioned the death to someone as he passed, and by the magic of the mountain grapevine the news was spreading rapidly. Neighbors began to arrive. The men went to the barn to make a coffin and a box to lay Grandma away in, while some of the women went into the kitchen to make a dress suitable for her burial and others went into the bedroom to "lay her out." Her husband and her daughters had no part in any of this. All was done by willing friends.

They bathed her and combed her hair. They put coins on her eyes to hold the lids closed and tied a cloth around her chin to hold it up until the features were set. They covered her face and hands with cloths moistened in camphor, to keep them white. When the new dress was ready it was put on, and the old body was placed in the new coffin.

When a man dies he is bathed and shaved by the men. There may be clothing on hand which can be used for him, but a woman must usually have a new dress.

If the Justices had lived nearer to a town they might have bought a casket and box. The store would have delivered them to the house in a truck or wagon and later would have taken the body to the cemetery. Or the Justices might have carried burial insurance and had all of the arrangements for the funeral cared for by a burial association. Many mountaineers have this form of insurance.

A one-hundred-dollar burial policy can be carried for twenty-five cents a quarter for an adult. There are policies for children at fifteen cents a quarter. Seventy-five cents a quarter pays for a three-hundred-dollar policy. This provides for the body to be taken into town for embalming. Under the other policies there is no embalming. The undertaker goes to the home to prepare the body for burial.

But even if these services had been available Grandma would probably have preferred the home-made coffin.

More neighbors came. The graveyard was miles away, so the burial could not take place till next day. These friends were coming to sit up with the family that one night while Grandma was still above ground. The old body would not be left alone

nor in the dark for an instant until it was laid
lovingly in the box and put safely to rest underground, for its spirit must not be lonesome nor
neglected nor disturbed—and the huge mountain
rats are ravenous.

They spent the night in drinking much hot,
strong coffee and recounting old stories to keep
themselves awake until the funeral procession
could get started at break of day.

Before daylight one wagonload of men went
ahead to dig the grave. They had not gone the
evening before because it is considered bad luck to
leave a grave open overnight. They took the box
with them.

As the funeral procession went over the rough
road to the graveyard several of the men rode in the
back of Ted's wagon, steadying the coffin as best
they could so that it would not turn over or bounce
out. They went slowly. The burial must not take
place until after noon.

The graveyard was in a clearing on top of a
hill. There was a fence around it to exclude animals, but there was no evidence of other care. The
graves were weed covered. Some were sheltered by
wooden roofs, some with huge slabs of stone. One
small grave was bordered with inverted fruit jars.
Under each was a child's plaything. Many of the
headstones had fallen down. It was a bleak, for-
saken, comfortless place.

There was a prayer at the graveside, and a
hymn sung by the mourners, but no further service. No minister could be got on short notice at
this time of year, and in the mountains there must

be quick burial, when there is no undertaker and no embalming. When a circuit rider came through the hills in the spring, there would be a day of services at the cemetery for all those who had died since his last visit, with lengthy eulogies, and a basket lunch.

After the last clod of dirt had been thrown into the grave the Brogdons went home with the Justices, to help set the house in order.

"Let us take Gran'paw with us till you sorter git on your feet," John offered.

"Thank 'e kindly, but he's like to be more content here where she was," Ted declined.

Grandpa was unquestionably a pawn, with his moves determined by others, but, fortunately, he was in the hands of considerate players.

In the late afternoon the Brogdons started back across the mountain to their own home. They had done all they could.

Sarah worried about the depleted food supply which was left to Addie and Ted.

"Shucks shuckins! I wisht you'd a seed Ted's smokehouse. He ain't hardly got no meat left, and all of us there a-eatin' him out of house 'n' home."

But they knew that if there were similar illness at the Brogdons' or the Combses', the Justices would take their children and go to the afflicted ones just as quickly.

As they bumped along, the shadows of the tree trunks stretched out across their way, like hurdles.

13

Jest A-Chewin' the Rag

There was a man who had no eyes,
He went abroad to view the skies;
He saw a tree with apples on it,
He took no apples off, yet left no apples on it.

THREE MEN SAT NEAR THE STOVE AT THE BACK OF A crossroads store. One sat on a keg, one on a box, and one on an old chair held together with wire. It was Sunday afternoon. Rain was pouring down outside. Only a little thin gray light got into the room, strained through the dust on the high window. But the spot near the stove was warm, a cheery glow of firelight flickered through the crack in the stove door, and the men were content to sit thus, cozily, and talk.

Rob Foster spoke. He had vivid blue eyes, the blazing blue of a hot summer sky. They were piercing eyes. His look seemed to dart out of them. "You-all hear 'bout the shootin' up to Brewers'?"

"You mean Jess Young what's all the time hangin' around that Creecy Brewer woman? I allers said like as not if her old man ever come home and found Jess there, they's liable to be a shootin', or leastways a fraction," Lige Johnson spoke. His left arm was amputated near the shoulder. With a show of satisfaction that his prognostication had proved correct, he fished a plug of tobacco out of the depth of a right-hand pocket, held it under the stump of an arm, and carefully cut off a piece, which he stuffed into his cheek. Lige always knew that the worst would happen.

" 'Twarn't Jess," Rob corrected him. " 'Twas that Willie Davis done it, him as got sent up fer thievin' from Silas's store."

"That's how come Creecy had them new shiny shoes and that silk bed kiver, I heerd," Lige put in.

"What about the shootin'?" Bud Goforth prompted.

"Well, Willie Davis he got out of the jailhouse and up and made smack dab fer the Brewers'. (Some says they was in on the thievin' and should of ben sent up too.) He laid low at their place fer a time and then someone told the law he was there."

"I bet it was Jess or old man Brewer, one, got tired of him hangin' 'round Creecy," Lige conjectured.

"Sheriff went up there last evenin' and yelled fer Willie to come out or he'd go in. Nothin' happened so he went through the gate and started fer the door. Jest then Willie come around the end of the house, pushin' Creecy in front of him. The sheriff couldn't shoot fer fear of hittin' her. Willie let loose his gun 'round her and kilt the sheriff where he stood. Then he took off fer the woods on Brock Mountain to hide out and hain't ben found, leastways not last I heerd, though a posse's ben huntin' ever sence."

"That was a good sheriff too. Good's this county's ever had," Bud mourned. "Why didn't we handle it our own selves when Willie was caught stealin'? I wanted to go burn him out, but Silas sent fer the law, and now it's fruited in the killin' of a good man. The law cain't do nothin'. Why don't we keep on settlin' things our own selves same as we allers did?"

Bud was the youngest of the three men, in years, but there was no correlation between his years and his opinions. Some men are born old—faithless and pessimistic—just as others, regardless of age, never lose the power to see visions of better things. Bud was "agin everything." He wasn't perverse. He was sincerely afraid that, terrible as things are, the last vestige of civilization would crumble with any change in the status quo.

"Law ketched him, didn't it?" Lige wanted to argue.

"Shore. But it couldn't hold him, could it?" Bud retaliated. "Hit ketched Noah Qualls too, both times he kilt a man, and let him go both times, and he's scot free to this day—him as ort of ben massacreed."

"You know them Quallses. Their whole tribe has such tempers they go wild if you make 'em mad. They wouldn't a juror's life a ben wuth a cent," Rob reminded him.

"Burnin's helps, or ridin' on a rail," Lige agreed with Bud.

"A firy cross would be too good fer Noah Qualls," Rob was emphatic.

"You mean like they used on Oliver Hensley over to Ruddell Gap?"

"Yep. Noah is worser 'n Oliver, easy."

"I was down to my sunnin'-law's then, helpin' 'em pick cotton. What happened?" Lige asked.

"We could see the fire a fur piece across the hills from our place," Rob recalled. "I says to my woman, 'Looks like that might be one of them crosses I've hearn tell about,' s'I. 'Hit do, fer sartin,' says she. So I calculate I'll mosey over and see fer my own self.

"I rode my critter till I was close. Then I hobbled him and snuck on through the bresh so's not to meet no one. I reckoned they most likely warn't lookin' fer company.

"I got clean up to the clearin' afore I found there warn't nary man there. Don't much believe they'd heerd me. Reckon by the looks of things it was over. But the big cross of logs was standin' up a-burnin' bright, and there was a sight of wood had ben piled and burned around the bottom."

"Had they burned Oliver on the cross?" Lige was avid.

"I couldn't rightly tell. They was somethin' dark amongst the wood what was still glowin'. But I've hearn it said they only burnt his hands and feet till he promised to clear out, and jest used the cross to skeer him."

"Anyhow, he ain't never ben seen sence. That's sartin," Bud concluded.

"The law maybe didn't keep Noah Qualls, but the government *is* doin' some good with this release work," Rob commended.

"Some as gits it needs it and some don't," Bud was caustic. "You-all know what Neal Allwhite's

Outside a crossroads store

Tranquillity

A church house

Dinnertime

A "bresh arbor"

woman told that government lady when she went
to visit 'em? Neal, he's a purty good sorry feller,
and a big windjammer, but his woman says, 'My
hosband, he's disabled to work. Why, lady, he
couldn't do a day's work if he was goin' to die in a
minute." Bud mimicked her in a squeaky fal-
setto. "What she should of said was he *wouldn't* do
no work, he's that lazy. Jest wears out the seat of
his trousers a-settin' on goods boxes here. If her or
him either ever told the truth it would be a
accident."

"Mebbe some gits it as shouldn't," Rob conceded.
"But they's others what's on starvation what won't
take it. I ben a-tellin' old Gran'maw Flinn that
she'd orter ax, but she allers makes answer in her
own homely way, 'I don't keer what the rest of 'em
says, I say when you are give groceries that's
charity, and I hain't never took charity all my life,
and I don't aim to start at my age,' says she. 'If I
could work that would be different, but I ain't
a-takin' no free help, although I reckon I got as
good a right to it as any, fer I give to the Red Cross
once and they told me if I ever got in trouble they'd
help me out. I'll manage on eggs and milk,' says
she. And her bein' like to starve don't budge her."

"Ol' Gran'maw Flinn's proud and sot in her
ways," Bud agreed. "She might near blowed up
when someone named it to her about that school
over yon mountain what showed a pitcher of a kid
in tore overhauls and no shoes, on a paper they
sent outside to ax fer money to help 'our pore
mountain brothers.' You-all know no kids don't
go to that school a-lookin' that-a-way, and 'twarn't

right to pitcher 'em like they did. What'll folks think we are, anyhow!"

"Government don't do that-a-way, nohow. Hit's ben treatin' us like white folks," Lige said. "Only thing much I knowed about it afore was that it was at a place called Washington, and it took some of our boys away somewheres to fight some furriners they had nary grudge agin, when they'd a heap sight ruther of stayed to home as ter go."

"My gran'pappy fit the damnyankees in the War," Bud bragged. "The war" is still the Civil War, and "damnyankee" is still all one word.

"What I hain't liked about the government is the way it sends revenuers in here to hunt fer stills," Lige complained. "What business is it of its what we do with our corn?"

Distillation of liquor, and its consumption, is considered a prerogative rather than a moral question by the mountaineers. The fact that liquor is involved in most of the shootings and fights and troubles of other sorts does not cause them to relegate it to the category of moral issues, any more than it does many of their city brothers.

"I used to think that was all the government was good fer," Rob admitted, "but I've thought more kindly of it sence it's ben a-tryin' to help us."

To many to whom the government had been only a troublesome watchdog, it has now become a benign agent which is seeking to alleviate suffering and misery.

"I wisht, 'stead of huntin' fer stills, it would make that Dowell Williams, what lives next down from my girl's place, quit drinkin'," Lige sug-

gester. "All that tribe of Williamses is drinkers,
and I misdoubt but Dowell's worser 'n any. He's
ben carried home drunk twice this week a-ready.
And he's sick all the time, too. He got a-holt of
some poison liquor when he was a kid and he's got
snakes in his boots."

"Had you heerd that after his old man died,
Mis' Williams was puttin' the pillow feathers in
new ticks one day and found a feather crown in the
pillow the old man's head was a-layin' on when he
died?" Bud asked. "Haw, haw," he roared. "Him
with a feather crown! Hain't that the beatin'est!
Hit jest goes to show there ain't nothin' in that
there say-so."

Rob's eyes flashed, and even Lige seemed
shocked. "Don't talk that-a-way, Bud," Rob
warned. "They's damnation fer them as mocks
the Almighty. You must not of heerd that they
figgered back and recollected that their least one
had died on that same pillow."

The feather-crown superstition is an old one
in the hills. When a person dies, his bed pillow
may be ripped open to see if, perchance, his life
has been so holy and pure that he has had a crown
to leave behind, in addition to the one he took to
Glory. Very rarely, but often enough to perpetu-
ate the belief, there is found a matted mass of the
softest and finest feathers, rolled tightly about one
another into a flat crown. Occasionally, as in the
case of Mr. Williams, the finding of a feather
crown in the pillow of the departed one comes as
a surprising revelation to the members of the
family, who had had no cause to suspect his out-

standing virtue, but in that event it is often possible to recall that some other person more deserv-
ing of the crown had previously breathed his last
on the same pillow, and the mystery is cleared
away. These rare crowns are preserved assiduously and regarded with awe by the survivors.

"You'd ought to be goin' to the revival over to
Maple Grove, Bud Goforth, and git yourself set
right with God," Rob admonished.

"I hain't got no church clothes," Bud made ex-
cuse.

"Don't matter," Rob assured him. "The Lord
looketh on the heart."

"Yeah. But the folks what's there looketh on
the outward appearance," Bud rejoined.

"Them clothes you got on's good enough," Lige
said. "Folks is comin' in what they got."

"Has they ben a big crowd?"

"Last night I'd a-swore nigh onto everybody was
there," Lige said. "They reckoned the church
house wouldn't hold 'em, so they'd put up a bresh
arbor. 'A-meetin' in a tabernacle made with
hands,' preacher says. He kin shore quote Scrip-
ture!"

"Crowd shore got het up last night," Rob's voice
reflected some of the excitement. "Preacher read
from the Good Book, and had us sing a bunch of
songs. (Gid taken his guitar fer us to sing by.)
Then drekly he told about how the pains of Hell
would gat hold upon us if we didn't repent and be
saved.

"Newt Arms' oldest boy, Knox, is goin' on fifteen. He wanted to be saved but he couldn't see no

light. Then preacher told us all to pray. He kinda
beat time and led off, and we all prayed, over and
over, 'Oh, Lord, save him!'

"Preacher says to the boy, 'You'll have to wrassle
with the Lord,' and the kid wrassled there till he
was plumb gin out and all over bruises and pump
knots. His maw wrassled too, and they went down
to spell 'em off, their friends, though we couldn't
see who they was a-wrasslin' with," Lige said.

" 'You cain't see God and live,' " Rob quoted.

"Preacherman said our faith was weak was why
the boy couldn't git religion, and we'd got to pray
harder, 'stead of peterin' out. He got us to swayin'
in time to the prayin', 'Oh, Lord, save him!' Some
was took so by the Holy Spirit that they fell on the
ground and rolled and jerked. Matt Green got to
talkin' in tongues. Preacher says it was a message
of help and encouragement, but young Arms
couldn't understand. He had eyes but couldn't see,
and ears but couldn't hear.

"We done our level down best and finally preacher says we'd done all we could fer one night, so
we's to all go home and carry Knox on our hearts
till meetin' time today, and then we'd try agin.
But they won't be no meetin' today, by the looks
of this plaguey rain, so we'll have to go on a-car-
ryin' him, and him stay out of the fold, till it stops,"
Rob concluded regretfully.

"What bothered the boy was the preacher sayin'
that them as is converted sins no more," Rob recalled. "Knox held he knows folks what's got religion what sins. Preacher quotin', 'We who died
to sin, how shall we any longer live therein?' didn't

budge him one smidgin. The preacher says, 'There
ain't no argyment. You're a-strainin' at a gnat.
Ax the Lord to help you strain it clean out.' "

"Hit's folks like that Etta Hawkins what makes
the young-uns mistrust," Bud worried. "Hit's
knowed she got religion once, and take a look at
her now! Clarence, he was a-makin' out all right
and makin' a right good livin' till she hooked him.
Now she won't let him out'n her sight fer fear he'll
run after some other woman, she's that jealous.
And he ain't that sorter feller! He's a good boy
who wouldn't think to do such a thing—as she
could see if she warn't so plaguey jealous. But
she won't leave him go fishin' or shell diggin' less'n
she's along, and she's might nigh ruint him
aready."

Lige jumped in gleefully. "As if she had room
to talk! Hit's said she lives dishonorably. I would-
n't want to say. But I do know that her and Ethel
Hix went into town the other day on the train.
Most folks walks if they cain't ride theirselves.
How they got the money to go in I wouldn't say.

"I seen her a-comin' home. The train gitten
into that little station five mile from her place at
seven o'clock at night and she didn't show up to
home till the next mornin', with her arms full of
groceries."

"They ain't a word of truth in that, Lige!" Rob
corrected him. "Ethel Hix told me about that trip
her own self. She says it was dark when the train
come in, so they hid their grub in a empty shack by
the tracks and went on home. You know Ethel
lives along that deep ravine and Etta has to cross

the swamp. Hit was slow goin' along in the dark.
Ethel didn't git home till way along in the middle
o' the night and Etta lives further 'n her. Next
mornin' Etta went back early, she says, to beat
somebody else to their stuff, and toted hern and
Ethel's home, too."

"That's what *she* says," Lige sneered. Uncon-
vinced, he could think of no more convincing re-
joinder. His mind was muddy with the dirt it had
stirred up, so his thought was sluggish.

"Preacherman sent word to Etta that she's like
to go to torment if she don't come to preachin',"
Rob conceded.

Bud changed the tenor of his complaint. "Did
you know that Grace and Glory woman preacher
what was here last, was a-livin' with her fourth
man?"

"I hearn tell she was," Lige answered, "and I
heerd why. She says, 'The laborer is worthy of his
hire,' so she sets and reads or thinks or jest sets,
while her menfolks cook and wash the dishes and
the clothes and clean the house. I figger it don't
take much of that to skeer 'em off if they got bay
horse sense."

"And that ain't all," Bud went on. "I heerd on
good say-so that she let her valise out a window at
the hotel in town and then walked out without
payin' her bill. If that's a lie you got it as cheap
as I did."

"I reckon she'd ben a-thinkin' of how Saul got
out of Damascus by bein' let down over the wall in
a basket," Rob chuckled.

In being deceptive the "lady preacher" was an

exception. Most of these spiritual shepherds are honest, and terribly, heartbreakingly sincere.

The talk moved on to points of doctrine. Mountaineers glory in discussing the abstract and the obscure. Removed from its context some striking passage will catch the imagination and afford material for endless exegesis, debate, and local interpretation, often with amazing results. Passages such as the following, considered by themselves, prove stimulating: "In my name shall they cast out demons; they shall speak with new tongues; they shall take up serpents, and if they drink any deadly thing, it shall in no wise hurt them; they shall lay hands on the sick, and they shall recover." The creation, Jonah, the miracles, Revelation, all are sources of favored topics.

Rob and Lige and Bud stayed close by the cheery fire, arguing and wondering and making positive assertions on points that have remained enigmas to the sages of the world from time immemorial, until it was chore time and they had to go home.

14

The Character of the Mountaineer

I went into the woods, and built me a kirk.

THE MOUNTAINEERS HOLD TO THEIR INDEPENDENCE
as to a priceless heritage. It is shown in their re-
sentment of revenue officers who try to tell them
what they shall not do with their corn; in their dis-
approval of Rural Rehabilitation administrators
who tell them what they shall plant and where they
shall plant it; in their distrust of county medical
officers who say they shall have their children
vaccinated; in their unwillingness to move into a
town, where laws and close neighbors will curb
their freedom; and in their dislike of "public
works," which are not only road and bridge construction and other state and county jobs, but also
any sort of employment in which a man works for
a boss, for a weekly wage, and may be fired at the
discretion of the man who hired him. They cling
tenaciously to their independence.

They cling also to their heritage of self-satisfac-
tion. They still loyally believe that the ways of
their forbears were the best ways. They are ultra-
conservative. And what a comfortable stand that
is; to be positive about the things one believes, not

to be open to doubt, and thereby to spare oneself the turmoil and disagreeable uncertainty of weighing alternative possibilities and making decisions. The conceiving of a new idea is painful.

But their conservatism is not simply evasion, it is also self-preservation. They have inadequate bases for differentiating the proven from the hypothetical, the true from the quack. Knowledge has grown gradually around them while they have sat undisturbed and satisfied with their old convictions. When it does get in to them now, it reaches them in lumps—boulders of fact put down in their midst without any carefully built foundation on which to rest.

They privately question a little their ability to cope with unfamiliar things. They feel safer in their rut. They want to be left alone. They resent any implication that the time-honored ways are not the best, or that they should be supplemented or supplanted. And so they have raised a wall of mistrust and aversion to change to protect themselves against it.

No people can stand still. If they are cut off from sources of information, retrogression is inevitable, for the old store of wisdom will decrease. It is impossible, by word of mouth, to pass on all of the knowledge one has received. Some will unavoidably escape, and the total will gradually diminish. Lost skills which are not essential to life in the wilderness, such as the ability to read the Latin books which are occasionally found tucked away in a mountain trunk or loft, are simply gone. Lost wisdom which is needed for the meeting of recurring problems, such as the correct method for treating certain illnesses, is replaced by homemade theories, and the awareness of any loss is soon dispelled.

Their ancestors, those early pioneers of our country, were an independent people whose roots in the sure *here* was not as strong as the pull of the unknown *there*. They turned their backs on civilization and security and ease, in order to have elbow room and freedom to manage their own affairs, undisturbed by close-pressing neighbors. They learned to supply themselves with food and clothing and all of the necessities of life, almost unaided by the inaccessible world they had left behind. They settled their own disputes, worked out their own precepts, and became a law unto themselves. And having done all this, having won their independence, they looked on their accomplishment and were justly proud. The new country they had chosen was a good land. Their ways had proved to be good ways. They had demonstrated their self-sufficiency and they were satisfied.

Their descendants have been left behind as the world around them, having maintained its contact with the sources of information, has moved on. They lack the fearless courage, the driving initiative, and the impelling curiosity that brought their ancestors to this far country. Their present methods do not result in the success which warranted the self-esteem of their forefathers. But unmindful of loss, they have held tight to their self-esteem.

Mountain pride is a powerful thing, strong

enough in some people to make them starve rather than ask for aid. It breaks down sooner in the parents of young children. They apologize, "We ben gittin' by as skinny as we could. We never would of ast only the least ones was plumb naked fer clothes and a-cryin' with honger."

For a long time in our country, we have had the idea, and properly so, that the recipient of charity was either mentally subnormal, physically unfit, or morally deficient. The mountaineer has been of the same opinion. As a result of the depression, self-respecting persons to whom any of these epithets were entirely unsuited, found themselves dependent, through no fault of their own. The mountaineers were slow to acknowledge this, and even when they themselves were forced to admit it because they became destitute, they were afraid that their neighbors would not understand that it was not their fault.

Even yet there are some persons, willfully blind in the face of facts, or pitifully ignorant, who superciliously assert that anyone with initiative and ingenuity can get a job—but their number is few, for most people by this time have had relatives or friends who needed assistance.

The man "on relief" often has too much time to think and too much time for introspection. He becomes supersensitive in his contacts with his fellowmen and may attribute to them derogatory opinions about himself and his circumstances of which they may be entirely innocent. Into careless remarks of theirs he may read significant and pride-shattering meanings of which they never dreamed. Standing in line in a relief office or a commissary, or presenting stamps for groceries to his old family grocer, is not soothing to a man in this mental condition.

By far the majority of families who have found it necessary to ask for help, preferred work relief to direct relief, avoided requesting direct relief as long as possible, and were ashamed to ask when it became necessary. A man would explain, "I've worked all my life and never asked ary man fer help. I'm able bodied and I'm willin'. Me and the woman'd a heap ruther have work, both of us. We feel disgraced, seems like, a-havin' to ask fer help. We don't want nothin' if we don't deserve it. We've begged fer some sort of work—any sort that would let us care fer our own———anythin' honorable, that is—but jobs is mighty skeerce. We've managed best we could, but it's ben mighty sorry at times."

Gradually, after circumstances had forced them to seek aid, the stigma of going to the relief office lessened for some of them, as more and more of their neighbors went also. It became quite the correct thing, this biweekly trip to town. At first they joked about it in an effort to suggest that they did not care. Later some of them joked about it because they really did not. They have been saved from starvation, but the insidious, enervating results of paternalism have gradually affected many of them. When they submitted to the necessity of taking relief, their morale was definitely lowered, and their pride was broken. Time and wisdom will be needed to mend it.

Their environment has played a great part in

the development of the mountaineers' philosophy.
They are fatalistic. When the first hillsmen came
across the country there was an abundance of rich
land. A man could farm as he wished and, when
the richness of his land was impaired, he could
move on. The Ozarks were fertile when the first
settlers came. But as families stayed and used the
same land repeatedly instead of moving farther,
the soil became impoverished and its yield gradually lessened.

What was a man to do? Soil conservation had
not been an issue with his ancestors and they had
bequeathed him no maxims helpful in dealing with
this new problem. And so he placed the responsibility on God—"acts of God." Flood and drouth,
wind and boll weevil, good crop and poor, what
could a man do about them! He could plant and
tend and gather, but the increase he must leave to
God. His ancestors had waited for harvest time
with faith and assurance. He just waited. And he
still waits.

He does try occasionally to sway the decisions of
the Almighty. He does his planting when the moon
is right, that is, he plants potatoes, onions, and
other crops which grow underground, in the dark
of the moon. Crops which bear the edible part
above ground, such as beans and corn, he plants in
the light of the moon. He digs his potatoes in the
light of the moon to keep them from rotting. The
almanac is very important to his plans. He dis-
credits the theory of increasing yield by the use
of fertilizer.

He counts the number of stars within the circle

around the moon to know how many days will elapse before he can rightfully expect rain. In case of drouth he may kill a snake and stretch it on the ground with its ventral side turned toward the sky, and then wait three days to see if his offering does not win for him the needed rain. Terracing to preserve moisture is a newfangled idea to him—if he has heard of it at all.

Having done what he can, he waits. What must be will be.

The highlander is often accused of shiftlessness. It is true that he is not overfull of exuberant energy. Houses may long remain unfinished. A porch may lack roof or floor. There may be a door with no doorstep. After the family has become accustomed to jumping out and climbing into the house, there is a tendency to forget that a step had ever been intended. A family whose house has burned down may remain for years in inadequate temporary quarters which were to have sheltered them only for a few days. It is no uncommon thing at any time of the day to find the men of the family seated flat on the porch with their backs against the wall, or lounging on broken chairs before the fire, while their fences and gates remain decrepit, the roof leaks in a dozen places, outhouses list precariously, and the chickens, lacking shelter, roost in trees.

But it would perhaps be better to call this inertia rather than shiftlessness. A powerful force is required to stir the mountaineer to unusual exertion. He is the product of generations of intermarriage, which has not increased his vitality or vigor. He has learned though bitter experience that his self-

directed efforts are of little avail against the inex-
orableness of his environment, and this idea has so
permeated his thinking that it colors his attitude
toward all the affairs of life. He feels that the results of his endeavor are seldom worth the trouble
they required. Days are long and the year is long.
There will be tomorrow and more tomorrows. Why
make life harder by crowding it?

He is not resentful toward life. Long years of
hardship have taught him to endure unresistingly.
He has learned patience. He goes quietly on doing
what is to be done. He has no faith in new ways
but he tries the old ones again and again and again.
Habit is strong in him. He does what he has always
done and what his father did before him. If a crop
is good he pays his bills but he does not get excited;
the crop next year may be poor. If the crop is poor
his bills are not paid, and he eats a little less and
patiently waits for another year when it may be
better.

He lives in the midst of beauty and he takes
pleasure in it in a passive way because he is accustomed to it. If he goes out of the hills he appre-
ciates what he has left behind. Trees are missed in
a treeless country, and a flat country, where the
sun rises from the level land, is unfinished, like a
picture without a frame.

He has leisure and he enjoys it. The bustle and
hurry of the outside world are incomprehensible
to him. Why should people want to rush so? He has
no meetings, no appointments. He has time to stop
in the midst of his early morning chores to glory
in the sunrise. He can pause in the midst of his

plowing to watch colts romping in an adjoining field. At dusk he is free to sit in his yard and hear night settling down. During harvest he sees the birds wing southward. At any time he will stop to notice weather signs. Croaking frogs, articulate fowl, clouds, sunrise, and sunset all have messages for which he is waiting. He takes time to talk with family and friends, not in alphabetic abbreviations, but slowly, deliberately, and at length. Or he sits with them in comfortable tranquil silence.

The even flow and conventionality of mountain life is relaxing to an outsider who has become accustomed to being keyed to the unexpected.

Mountaineers are ordinarily calm and undemonstrative. Their hands remain quiet when they speak, and their voices seldom indicate animation or stress. But when they are stirred by some powerful feeling they may react violently, actuated by emotion untempered by reason. Their passion, habitually suppressed, seems to seethe and then erupt under sufficient pressure. This pressure may come in the guise of religion.

The frequency and regularity of church services depends upon the availability of a preacher. If he lives and farms in the locality he may hold regular services in three or four churches, giving them his Sundays in rotation. On their Sunday the people of each congregation will go to church, with their dinners in baskets, and stay for an all-day meeting. A resident pastor will also help his people in case of trouble or illness or death. He will conduct funerals and weddings. There are a few such devoted men serving the mountaineers. Theirs are not the meetings at which the emotional floodgates are opened. They remain with their congregations for a longer time than such feeling can be sustained.

But many communities do not have this type of ministration offered them, and to them, as well as to the communities already receiving some spiritual guidance, come itinerant preachers and evangelists. During July or August, when there is a lull in the farm work, they will hold a.meeting each evening for a week or two in one vicinity, and then move on to another.

Formerly it was Methodist or Baptist circuit riders who came to hold annual camp meetings near a spring or a stream. As might be expected, the religious concepts of the mountain people are infused with superstition. Here is rich soil for sects appealing primarily to the emotions. Now the revivalists who come to them are more often Pentecostals—Oneists, or Council or Free—or Holiness people, perhaps, or Grace and Glory adherants, or representatives of less-known denominations.

A missionary home on furlough from the heart of Africa remarked, after attending a Holy Roller revival meeting in these mountains, "These people have religion in abundance, but what a religion! Never in all of Africa have I seen the display of more rabid fanaticism."

Frequently there is no church building in the community, or the crowds are too large for the church. Then the men in the neighborhood put up a framework of tree posts in the woods, roof it with leafy branches, roll in logs or bring planks for seats, make a rough table for a pulpit and have a "bresh arbor" ready for the people. Families come from all around, tie their horses to near-by trees, and enjoy the service.

The preachers, ordinarily with a degree of educational attainment just a step higher than that of their audiences but endowed with great eloquence, tell vividly of fire and brimstone, calling upon their hearers for repentance and testimonials. Their god is not a loving, seeking god. He is a wrathful god to be appeased, a jealous god to be wheedled, albeit he is a just god who will sit in judgment upon the world at the last trump. It seems easier for a people who have suffered long to understand hell-fire than the love of God.

The mountain folk are often stirred to frenzy by such preaching. It may shatter their usual taciturnity and put them writhing and groaning in the aisles. The rumor of a wrong done may send them out on a mission of violent justice. Sometimes atrocities are committed against some erring brother, in the sincere belief that the avenger is obeying a miraculously received command. Rumors of scourgings, and torture and even murder done in the name of the Lord, as directed in a vision or a trance, seep out of the hills.

Ordinarily there are no such dire results. For many of the people these revivals are simply the most exciting occasions of the year, and when one is over they eagerly anticipate the next one.

Within a mountain neighborhood rumors travel fast. As with all underprivileged peoples who read and think little, gossip is rampant, as a fountain pen gushes when it is about to run dry. The mountain people have little to talk about except their neighbors.

The people of the Ozarks have their own ways of enforcing their code. Both men and women may be pitiless when they are persuaded that a wrong has been done, but they are not always sure to verify the facts before judging.

The men are more prone to question the integrity than the propriety of a neighbor, but are no less inclined to gossip about it than are the women. If they hear, and become convinced, that he has stolen some food or cotton or has cut a fishline, he may find his barn in flames some night. If he gets a generally bad reputation he may be ridden out of the neighborhood on a rail and warned not to return. Both are common methods of evincing popular indignation. Such reports may be spread with especial rapidity about a family from "outside" which has tried to insinuate itself into a community.

Fire is a favorite instrument of punishment. The members of some families never all leave home at one time because they know that someone has reason to want to rid the neighborhood of them.

Not all burnings are punishments. A family with a clear conscience may never leave their home unprotected. If they have a neighbor who is angry or jealous or dishonest they may fear that he will burn down their house or barn or steal their food if they all go away.

A man who has undesirable tenants in a house he owns, must be tactful in removing them. If he sends them away angry he knows that they may burn everything when they go, and leave him only his land.

Thieving and arson are seldom reported to "the law." If the offender is apprehended the chance of obtaining his conviction in court is slight. Retribution is more certain if the case is handled personally.

Even in more serious cases, such as assault or murder, the possibility of conviction is uncertain. The jurors know the defendant. Although they are sure of his guilt, if they feel that his crime is justified they will not convict. And they may not, even when they believe him wrong, if they fear him. He will leave a family to avenge himself if he is taken away, and if the law does not remove him permanently, he may return to have his own revenge.

Because so many cases are not reported to any authority it would be impossible to reckon the delinquency and crime in the hills. It can only be guessed that if it were calculable the record would not be one of which to be proud, if the legal definition of crime were held to. But remember that many acts which would be considered crime in a court of law are not so considered locally. They may be punishments, more effective than uncertain legal procedure, and be accepted as such by both prosecutors and defendant.

The women especially resent any violation or seeming violation of their moral standards or conventions, and may defame a neighbor's character on the most grossly misinterpreted circumstantial evidence. In the telling, the story of an indiscretion may grow to proportions entirely incomparable with the original facts. Then the whispers will fly behind the back of the condemned one until she begins to feel the coldness of her former friends. By that time the reports are so firmly believed that those who defended her at first may accuse her openly now, but denial on her part is likely to be given slight credence. She is finally assiduously avoided, and anyone who befriends her does so at the risk of her own position. On what a slender thread reputation hangs, so easily severed by a sharp tongue!

These methods of treating infringements have developed in a country where the people have become accustomed to being the law, with the preservation and welfare of their social structure dependent entirely upon themselves.

But mountain gossip is not all bad. The report of an unusual kindness done, or of a misfortune suffered, spreads as quickly as news of evil. The people go to help in case of need, more quickly than they go to punish in case of transgression. When illness or disaster or grief comes to a family, friends are on hand almost at once to supply help or advice or comfort or material assistance. A mountaineer would not care to exchange his loquacious neighborhood for the impersonality of a large city where, although his misdeeds would attract little attention, his adversity would be equally disregarded.

Ordinarily the hill folk are a friendly, neighborly people. Hospitality is traditional with them. In a land where hotels are far apart the wayfarer is taken in cordially even though the family may already overcrowd the house. They share what they have with him. When he leaves he may receive a jar of milk and some cold corn pone, "to piece on at midday," though the food supply may already be inadequate for their own needs.

Neighbors are always made welcome. There is much visiting among them—not just "pop-calls" but real visits—with a family going for the day and staying to dinner.

There is generosity. The man who has more peas or peaches than he needs will divide with a neighbor who has less.

Neighborliness is indispensable in a country where distance communication is slow. Neighbors are the first and often the only available help in case of need. They are sent for in sickness and birth and death. And they are called also for occasions of gaiety and celebration.

Family ties are strong in the mountains. Generations of a family have grown up in the same valley. The members know one another thoroughly, their strength and their weakness, their good and their bad points. And, knowing and understanding each other, and enjoying the aggrandizement of their own ego that comes from belonging to a family whose virtues are bright and whose faults are excusable, they stand stanchly by one another.

Intricate intermarriage has been inevitable in a country where the people ordinarily know no one living more than a few miles away. Families are interrelated in a most bewildering way. It is almost impossible for an outsider to grasp and remember all of the relationships. It is safer for him to take for granted that anyone may be related to anyone else, and not talk about anyone.

The mountaineer is frugal both from necessity and from choice. He knows that if he wastes what little he has he will pay for his folly with need more distressing. His wants are simple. He enjoys simple things. Our dissatisfactions are based on a disparaging comparison of the things we have with the things we might have or the things that others have. His satisfaction is based partly on the limitation of his field of comparison. The things he has and the pleasures that he has are as good, or nearly as good, as those of his neighbors. He is not made miserable by an insatiable desire for movies and modern plumbing and convenient kitchens and central heating. Just as we feel no lack of things which will be common to the next generation —even though we may have seen them pictured in a popular scientific magazine—so he feels no lack of these things which are outside the realm of his personal experience and are entirely unrelated to the everyday functioning of his own life. He does want food enough to eat, and clothing enough to cover him, and bedding enough to keep him warm, and a roof, and health, and life. And very often he cannot have even these minimal things.

15

Superstition

If you sneeze on Monday, you sneeze for danger;
Sneeze on a Tuesday, kiss a stranger;
Sneeze on a Wednesday, sneeze for a letter;
Sneeze on a Thursday, something better;
Sneeze on a Friday, sneeze for sorrow;
Sneeze on a Saturday, see your sweetheart tomorrow.

ONE INEVITABLE CONSEQUENCE OF ISOLATION, IN-
breeding, and ignorance is the prevalence and
strength of superstitions.

There are manifold superstitions in the mountains. It is probable that no one knows or believes
all of them. There are credulous persons who believe many. There are skeptics who believe few.
There are few, if any, who believe none. That is not
a trait peculiar to mountaineers. Everywhere there
are those who knock on wood to continue some good
fortune if they have inadvertently mentioned it,
and those who will not sit at a table with twelve
others.

A number of the superstitions clung to in the
mountains are also found elsewhere. Here again is
evidence of common ancestry—Elizabethan beliefs
brought to our country and scattered over it, but
preserved in purer form in the hill country.

The fear of black cats dates back to the days of

witchcraft. This was supposed to be a popular form for witches to assume in going about their nefarious business. Even today, to have a black cat cross one's path is considered an ill omen. If a strange black cat comes to a house it betokens good luck. But it is likely to be short-lived, for bad luck is in store if the cat leaves, or if he is allowed to stay. And it is useless to try to kill him, for he has eight more lives.

Weather signs are numerous in any section where success is dependent upon the weather. The mountaineer bases his prognostication upon sundry tokens for which he is always alert.

If the sun sets behind a bank of clouds on Sunday, there will be rain before the following Saturday, or even before the next Wednesday, according to some.

A cloudy sunset on Friday means rain before Sunday.

Bad weather is indicated by shooting stars, a yellow sunset, sensitive corns, or the old folks' rheumatism. And any mountain woman knows that if there is thunder the cream will sour.

There are divers signs to warn that rain may be expected soon. If the roosters crow at dusk, the sky is full of stars, or the lightning bugs fly low, it is well to bring in the trays of sliced apples which have been spread out to dry.

The call of the rain crow or the croak of tree frogs announce approaching rain. Other animals can sense its coming, too. Horses and cattle stretch their necks and sniff the air, and dogs eat grass. It may come from a sky which was rosy in the east at dawn or from a mackerel sky. An east wind will bring it.

The hillsman knows the old saying to be true that "All signs fail in dry weather," but he has ways of foretelling dry weather. If the whippoorwill calls, or an owl hoots in the barn lot, or the west wind blows, there will be no rain. Then will be the time for counting the stars within the circle around the moon, or, if this sign fails, for killing a snake.

Suppose an owl hoots when the east wind is blowing—contradictory signs. Then experience is important. Older people know best how to weigh such contrarieties.

There are indications of other prospective changes in weather. A rosy sunset means "fair and colder." When the wild geese fly south, cold weather is near. Frost will not come until the cosmos seed matures, but it is well to begin in August to listen for the first song of the katydid, for frost may be expected six weeks later.

There will be as many snows during the winter as the number of days the first snow stays on the ground.

The ground hog comes out of his hole in the Ozarks on February 2, to look at the weather. If it is clear and bright he goes back to his nest, but if he finds rain or snow he stays out, knowing that winter is over. The bear comes out on the second of February, too. If he sees his shadow he returns for six weeks more of sleep.

The ability to read weather signs is a great help to a farmer in planning the cultivation and harvesting of his crops. He has also been taught when to plant. Not only does he take care to plant crops bearing the edible part above ground in the light of the moon, and those which grow with the edible part below ground in the dark of the moon, but he finds it advisable to plant his potatoes on the hundredth day of the year (April 9 or 10), or on the seventeenth day of March, depending on which school of thought he sides with. The combined consideration of both date and moon phase may influence his decision. Bunch beans must go in on Good Friday, and lettuce must be sown on St. Valentine's Day. If February 14 falls on Sunday a man will have to arise very early to get his lettuce planted before daylight. But thus he may sidestep being seen at work on the Sabbath day.

A farmer may be spared much trouble if he knows the right signs and methods. A crowing hen forebodes trouble but makes an excellent stew, and the sooner the better. A dog can be kept at a new home by clipping some hairs from his tail and placing them under the doorstep. If the cow loses her cud, it may be restored by giving her a rag to chew. If she has "hollow horn" it can be cured by cutting a hole in her tail to let in some air. No informed mountain woman would set a hen on Sunday unless she wants all of the chicks to be roosters.

It is well to remember, if fish will not bite, to spit on the fishhook before it is dropped back into the stream.

There are numerous signs which will give valuable advance notice of coming events if one is watching for them.

An itching nose gives notice that company is coming, in time for a housewife to set her house in order. If she drops her dishrag she gets the same message. If her ears burn she knows that someone is talking about her, and her regret of past sins or her expectancy of future good is heightened. If she lets the bread burn she may prepare herself, for her husband is coming home in high dudgeon. Perhaps he smelled the burned bread.

A white spot on a fingernail signifies a trip which will start when the spot grows to the end of the nail—unless something interferes.

If a horseshoe is found on the ground it should be picked up and hung in a conspicuous place to insure good luck. One so displayed by someone else must not be removed or bad luck will follow for the one who removes it.

Those who know the signs can give advance information as to a baby's probable future.

A baby which cries a great deal will be a good adult, but a good baby will not live to be grown.

A pretty baby will become an ugly adult.

A child with long, thick hair cannot be expected to grow very fast, for all of its strength is going into its hair.

The third son will have the brains of the family.

A baby with long fingers or one which clasps a bit of money tightly in his little first will grow up to be wealthy.

If a baby smiles in his sleep it is because angels are talking to him. He probably will not live long.

There are many *don'ts*.

Don't start a journey on Friday.

Don't start anything on Friday which cannot be completed before Sunday.

After starting out, *don't* go back for something left behind. That brings bad luck. But if going on without the forgotten thing is impossible, the jinx may be averted by taking the first ten steps of the return journey backwards, with fingers crossed.

Don't button a new garment before it is worn.

Don't cut fence posts in the light of the moon. If this warning is disregarded the posts are sure to prove unsatisfactory.

There are *don'ts* connected with child care, in addition to those based on fear of prenatal marking or injury. *Don't* include a cap in a baby's layette. *Don't* cut his hair until he is a year old. If his fingernails are cut before the end of the first year he will be a thief. If he bites his nails he won't grow tall.

Don't let a baby walk before he has learned to crawl or he will never get very far.

If he sees himself in a mirror before he is a year old he will die before he is two.

A baby boy must not be tickled under the chin, for it will make him stutter. The same precaution is not necessary for a baby girl, for girls never stutter.

Don't carry a child over a stream with his head turned downstream or sooner or later he will be drowned.

Freedom of action about a house is greatly circumscribed. For fear of bad luck:

Ashes must not be carried out on Friday nor a rake, hoe, or plow taken into a house on any day.

(A housekeeper must have originated that one.)
A chair must not be whirled around on one leg nor
an umbrella opened indoors.

A wise person will not step over a broom nor
walk across the floor with one shoe off and one
shoe on, but he will take care to get out of bed
on the same side on which he got in or he will be in
bad humor all day.

It is bad luck to cut a doorway between two
rooms after a house is built. Recently some brave
souls have ventured to violate this rule. Others,
appreciating the resultant step saving, are daring
to follow their example.

Shingles should be rived in the dark of the moon,
for if they are split when the moon is waxing they
will warp.

It is folly to move from one house to another
when the moon is on the wane, but a move when the
moon is increasing will result in an increase of
prosperity for the family.

A dream must be told before breakfast if it is
to come true. Every dream has a meaning. It is
believed that one who is prepared to interpret them
correctly may be forewarned of many things.
Dream books are prized in the Ozarks.

Wishes, properly wished, may affect the future.
Some of the proper methods are:

Make a wish at the bottom of a hill, then don't
look back till the top is reached.

Make a wish and count twelve at the end of a
bridge, then walk across without speaking to anyone.

If a wish can be made when a redbird is seen

and completed before the bird flies away, it will come true. If the bird goes to the right when it leaves, the wish is doubly sure to come true. And a wish may be made on a flying crow if it does not flap its wings before it is out of sight.

If the same wish is made in any three of these ways, the hand of Providence is practically forced to do the wisher's will.

There are ways of accounting for some aches and illnesses, and there are aids to prevention for those who know.

If hair is cut in March, the head will ache the rest of the month. Of course it must not be washed in winter on pain of catching cold. Combings must not be dropped where birds can get them. The person whose hair is used in building a bird's nest will have a headache.

Night air is poisonous and should be shut out as much as possible. Although doors and windows are closed tightly at night, there are usually enough cracks in mountain-cabin walls to insure good ventilation.

If a disease is epidemic in the neighborhood it is thought well to wear, around the neck, a string to which is tied a small rag filled with asafetida. There it will be in convenient reach, to be chewed occasionally so that the disease may be warded off.

If a bag of salt is tied to a string around the waist when one has the mumps, other glands will not be affected.

There are many cures.

Consumption can be cured by wearing a penny on a string around the neck.

For earache, squeeze a bit of goose grease through a silk handkerchief into the ear.

Carry an Irish potato to relieve pain.

There are several methods of removing warts. Warts, by the way, may be caused by handling wart toads, or they may come quite inexplicably.

If a buyer can be found, a wart may be sold. The buyer, who pays the seller's price, will get the wart when it leaves the seller. Then he may profiteer by selling it for a higher price to someone else who will sell it in his turn.

If a buyer cannot be found, another means must be used. A silk thread may be tied around the wart. The patient must next be blindfolded and led three times around the yard. Blindfold and thread are then removed and the thread buried.

A wart may be given to an unsuspecting victim. The owner of the wart spits on it and rubs it with a piece of paper. This paper he folds and drops in the road. The wart will leave him and be transferred to the curious person who first picks up the paper.

Stop hiccoughs by holding the breath while taking nine swallows of water.

For nosebleed, raise a rock, spit under it, and replace the rock.

For chills, the patient should fasten a yarn string around a persimmon tree, tying as many knots as the number of chills he has had.

Rub a sprained ankle with vinegar.

If a man is a drunkard his wife may try feeding him scrambled owl's eggs.

If the desired results do not follow in any of these

cases, there has been a mistake in procedure, or faith is weak.

Baby's troubles are taken into consideration. When he is teething his gums may be eased by rubbing them with a live minnow and then tossing the fish back into the stream.

Thrush can be cured in one of two ways. Either give the baby a drink out of the heel of an old shoe, or find a man to blow in the baby's mouth. Some say it must be a man who has not seen the baby's father, and some say it must be a man who never saw his own father.

Both groups agree that in order to cure the hives it must be a parson who blows in the baby's mouth.

If a finger or toe, an arm or leg has been amputated and buried and, later on, the former owner suffers in that quarter, his suffering can be allayed only by digging up the buried appendage and settling it back more comfortably in its grave. Those who have experienced such pain say that they can feel the lost member as vividly as though it were still actually attached, and can get relief only when the aching part is "fixed" in the grave.

There are precautions to be taken in case of illness. Never sweep under a patient's bed nor make a new garment for a sick person. Don't shave or be shaved in bed.

To prevent night sweats, place a pan full of water under the bed. It must be full clear to the brim.

There are many superstitions associated with death and burial.

The howling of a dog at night is a portent of death.

After a death the body must never be left alone until it is buried safely away.

A grave must not be dug and left open overnight. There is time for the digging next morning, for were the burial accomplished before noon, another member of the family would die within a year.

Never wear a new dress or a new suit to a funeral, nor leave a graveyard until the last lump of earth has been thrown back onto the grave.

Avoid meeting a funeral procession if possible. Never count the wagons in a funeral procession. Crossing through a funeral procession is almost suicidal.

Never step over a grave nor lean on a headstone.

It is foolish to set out a cedar tree, for when it grows large enough to shade a grave the person who planted it will surely die.

After the funeral, a feather crown may be found, as a sign of the superabundant goodness of the departed one.

There are a great number of superstitions based on the love theme.

To see the reflection of the future mate, a girl or boy should look into the cistern on the first morning in May.

Another way to pry into the future is to go into the woods, find a flat rock, repeat a verse, and then lift the rock. Under it will be found a hair the color of that of the prospective life partner.

There are means, too, for learning whether one's love is returned, or whether a lover is true.

A girl may tie one end of a string around a Bible and attach the other end to a door key. While two of her friends support the dangling Bible, by holding the ends of the key, she will repeat: "And Ruth said: entreat me not to leave thee, or to return from following after thee: for whither thou goest, I will go; and where thou lodgest, I will lodge: thy people shall be my people, and thy God my God." As she ends the quotation she will repeat the name of the one she loves. If the Bible turns during this ceremony, it will indicate that the love is mutual.

If a mullen stalk, broken in the direction of the loved one's home, tries to rise again, it is a sign that the other one reciprocates.

A girl will draw one of her hairs between her fingers. If it curls she knows he loves her, if it does not curl he loves her not.

She may place a bit of love vine on a growing weed. If it flourishes, her lover is true, if it withers he is unfaithful. In that case she may make a powerful love potion by soaking her fingernail trimmings in whiskey. When her lover sips this, his affection for her will return.

If a man kindles a fire which burns brightly he knows that his sweetheart may be depended upon. But if the fire smolders and dies out he will take warning that someone else may be able to steal her love.

It is never safe for a couple to walk on opposite sides of a bush or tree when they are going down a path together. A violent quarrel is likely to follow such carelessness.

There are ghosts and "hants" in the Ozarks. A

Playing at the well

person who was born on Hallowe'en can talk with spirits and foretell many things, if he will.

A ghostly glow hangs over a cemetery. A door will not stay closed no matter how securely it has been fastened. Unaccountable footsteps are heard under the window or in the loft. There are "hanted" caves and hollows where only the ignorant or the foolhardy would wander alone. There is an irradiant snake which comes at night to give warning of impending danger.

A mountaineer has many ways of probing into the future, all of them just as informative and far cheaper than the urbanite's method of consulting an astrologer. But mountain superstition would be scoffed at as woefully ignorant, by the sophisticated city woman who lets the gypsy read her tea leaves, and who would not dream of living in an apartment numbered thirteen if one were to be found.

16

Conclusion

For every evil under the sun,
There is a remedy, or there is none.
If there be one, try and find it;
If there be none, never mind it.

NOT LONG AGO A PROMINENT SPEAKER IN A DISTANT state said something to this effect: "The problem of the American people today is no longer that of their pilgrim forefathers who struggled in the face of privation and illness to wring a meager subsistence from the New England soil. Our problem is not one of forcing nature to yield enough to sustain life. Our problem is one of disposing of the surplus. No longer must our people toil long hours to survive. Our labor-saving devices have done away with the need for laborers."

He may have been right to some degree, for the United States he knows and that which most of us know, but he was certainly not right as con-concerns great sections of our Ozarks and southern Appalachian Mountains, and many sections of the south-central United States. His statement was not true for the people in the Ozarks, struggling from the time they can walk till the day of their death to wring a scant existence from worn-out soil, with crops unsuited to the land, and without the benefit of labor-saving machinery. They have no surpluses and no leisure time to worry them. Some of them manage to make for themselves leisure, but that is not because there is nothing to do. It is because eventually the time comes when there seems to be little use in doing much.

We have touched strands of the people's needs, needs both chronic and of recent insistence. Let us gather them all together now.

We have found a general low standard of living in regard to such things as housing, conveniences, comfort, education, and culture. We have found that many things which much of the country considers necessities are considered in the mountains to be luxuries, or are even entirely unknown. All these conditions are of long standing and were as prevalent before the depression as they are now.

We have seen the physical needs. We have found some lack of food. We have found need for clothing and bedding and other things which, for their purchase, require cash or its equivalent in some sort of negotiable surplus. We have found much sickness, with a resultant need for medicine and medical care and knowledge. In the last few years the acuteness of these physical needs has been augmented for the mountain families by factors over which they have no control.

Long-time credit is a prime requisite for the amelioration of these needs. Without this the situation can scarcely be improved. Short-time loans at excessive interest are partly responsible for the present conditions. This long-time credit only the government has been able to offer. Any private agency or bank is in the loaning business for profit. The money is invested, and on the proceeds its owners are expecting to live. If they cannot get this living return from their wealth they will keep it themselves. The government, because it holds the confidence of its people, can borrow money for long terms at very low cost. It gets some by taxation. It can loan revenue thus procured for a long time, at little or no interest.

But credit alone is not enough for the mountain people. It would not be wise to put money into the hills to finance the raising of crops which are of little value, or which will overload the market. And it is not wise to spend money for farming to be done by poor methods, when it could be done more profitably by good ones. And so some agricultural direction and supervision must be supplied with the credit. This is being given with rehabilitation loans and will be furnished more extensively as this program grows. It could well be extended with credit of other sorts also. The agency which holds the purse is in a position to direct. No one who objects to such direction is required to borrow.

With improved farming methods the mountaineer should have time to clear more of his property and plant a greater acreage, and so have more produce to harvest and sell.

These people need to learn the uses to which their land may be put advantageously. They need to learn to give first space to food and feed stuffs in quantities sufficient for their requirements. They must learn that the hills are not all adapted to cotton. They can be taught that orchards and

vineyards would bring larger profits, and with
long-time credit they would be enabled to tide over
the time required for newly planted orchards and
vineyards to begin to bring returns. They can
learn that the hills are good for sheep and goat
raising, and for chicken and turkey farms. They
can learn to rotate crops and to clear land properly. And, incidentally, they can be taught that the
moon has no proved effect on potatoes and other
growing things.

Such knowledge is filtering into the hills gradually. County farm agents are working against op-
position. Some mountain boys who have got as far
as high school are getting the advantages of Smith-
Hughes training and 4-H Club work. The University experiment stations are being watched. But
most mountain farmers still lack ability to distinguish fact from fiction. Infiltration is a slow
process.

As more profitable crops are substituted for unprofitable ones now raised, the economic level
should rise. The need for credit should end as the
power to purchase things necessary to comfort and
health increases. Mountaineers, at present, are far
from having their share in the *commonwealth*.

There is an abundance of virgin land in the
mountains. If, upon investigation by experts, farm
land now being used were found worthless, it could
be abandoned or planted in trees and a family could
be moved to a better place. This virgin land would
have to be cleared, but with long-time credit a man
could take the time to clear it without the fear of
letting his family starve. Often this is the danger

which keeps him scratching at the submarginal land now, although the scratching brings him only enough to avoid this contingency.

But credit and improved farms and farming methods are not enough. No matter how much is raised it will be of little use if it cannot be got to market. Some sorts of produce could not be got to town in condition to sell, over the sorts of roads that lead from the more remote farms at present. A network of all-weather roads and of bridges over creeks which now can be forded only when they are low, is important. The creeks hold an abundance of suitable gravel for the roads. Much grading and stump pulling and boulder moving would be required, but if machinery were not available there is ample labor with ample time to do these things by slower methods. A start has been made toward meeting this need through government road-work projects, but it is only a start.

Good roads would make possible the greater development of natural resources.

Good roads would make possible much more regular school attendance on the part of many more children. A larger attendance would create a need for more schoolrooms. More schoolrooms would require more teachers. More literate children can become better farmers.

But child education is not enough. Adult education is needed also.

Both men and women need training in managing, in budgeting and buying, in sanitation, and in the importance of sufficient housing room.

The women need education in prenatal and child

care, home nursing, and isolation of communicable diseases. They need to learn the importance of food variation and the science of balanced diet, as well as the proper care of a house and more satisfactory and strength-saving laundry methods.

There is electric power along the highways that run through the mountains. The lines go past miles of homes without being tapped, because the people living there cannot afford the electricity or are ignorant of what it would do for them. These lines could be quickly extended to reach all of the hill country if there were sufficient demand for current. If not, there are local home-lighting units available for farm homes out of reach of electric lines. Even if they were able to afford such units at present, these people, if they know of them at all, through the educational influence of the mail-order catalog, think of them as entirely foreign to their own lives. Most of them never saw an electric range or an electric refrigerator in use. But the desire and the demand for modern things will come if the ability to satisfy it develops.

Some education for the use of leisure time is in order—some new interests more engrossing than loafing and gossiping. A supply of worthy thought food would benefit the whole people. Broadened interests and wider information would wake up many minds that have never had exercise nor an opportunity to stretch themselves, and these stimulated minds would turn themselves more profitably to all their problems.

As intellect develops, as reason supplants superstition and regulates the emotions, the religious emphasis of a people changes. As inevitably as educated missionaries establish schools in new territories to which they go, the good school, as its influence spreads, increases and elevates the spiritual understanding of the community. The love emphasis overbalances the fear emphasis. The prime interest shifts from unprofitable Biblical discussion to more worthy Christian living. As he becomes accustomed to thinking new thoughts the religious attitude of the mountaineer will change.

Until the economic condition improves considerably the mountains will still be mission territory. The church mission boards could help meet the present need if they were able to supply more and better-trained ministers and better-equipped church buildings.

Moral and spiritual development must keep step with mental development if these people are to realize the highest limit of their potentiality.

Improvement of conditions in the mountains will not be brought about by the people themselves. They cannot lift themselves by their own bootstraps.

The state of Arkansas can do little for them. In 1936 its per capita wealth was $770, with only one state, Mississippi, lower; while the per capita wealth of Nevada, which ranked highest, was $6,511, and the average for the United States was $2,293. According to the 1940 biennial report of the United States Office of Education, the average current expenditure for education for each elementary school pupil in average daily attendance during the year 1936, for twenty-two states

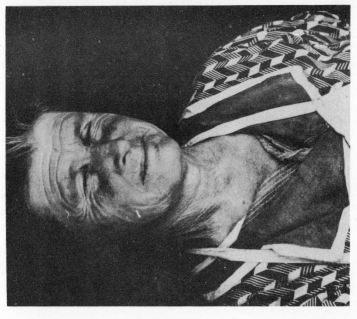

Farm Security Administration photograph by Shahn
Kindly eyes and a ready smile

Children at home

studied, was $57.69. The per student cost in Ne-
vada was $114.52. In Arkansas, which ranked
lowest, it was $18.76.

In most states where the need for general social
uplift of large numbers of people is the most acute,
the means for providing it are most lacking. The
Federal government is helping to meet this need.

There is nothing disgraceful about the way in
which the mountaineers live. Our great-great-
grandparents lived in the same way, and we consider them highly respectable.

When a people's entire energy is taken up with
the struggle to sustain life they have little opportunity to attain to a high degree of civilization.
There must be some economic leeway before the
standard of living can be raised. Some carefree
leisure time is necessary for the growth of culture.

The first settlers in the mountains needed all of
their time for the production of food. Their descendants settled into the rut of the old frontier life,
and in this life they have become static and im-
potent. They live in fear of fire, disease, dependent old age, and untimely death.

The cynic may suggest that there are features
of our so-called civilization without which they are
much better off. That is true, but the chance is that
he would not be willing to change places with a
mountaineer, even with one of the more prosperous
ones, any more than we would like to live as did
our great-great-grandparents.

Abraham Lincoln grew up in just such a cabin as
our Ozark mountaineers now occupy, but he was
great not because of his environment, but in spite

of it. The undernourished, overworked, ill-clad child does not have the best chance of developing the native ability or genius with which he may be endowed.

Mountain life is far from ideal, far even from the attainment of the highest as we know it. We believe, with all its faults, that we have found a better way of life; that we have a more abundant life to which these others have as much right, and from which they might be expected to derive as much benefit as we.

When a mountaineer is educated and placed in a modern social environment, his mountain mannerisms are soon polished off, although in the privacy of his own home he may still prefer beans and salt pork and corn bread. There are features of his mountain background which tend to make him a useful member of society. For there are some virtues found in the mountains which are rare outside —precious things worthy of careful preservation.

There is faith in God and man.

There is simple, unpretentious goodness. There are high moral standards which are looked upon as reliable and essential.

Mountaineers have contentment and joy in simple things. This could be so easily destroyed by creating a desire for the unattainable. As roads are built and outside forces infringe upon their seclusion, as is inevitable, may such desires be increased only as rapidly as they can serve as incentive, not rapidly enough to cause discouragement or despair.

The hillsmen have family unity and willing cooperation between generations. Education and modernization of the young, without a concurrent arousing of the older people from their lethargy, could snap this fragile link.

They have a love of independence. They want to be beholden to no man. The satisfaction of this desire has been eluding many of them.

They are generous and thrifty and honest, so they are good neighbors. They take time to cultivate friends and to be friendly. They take leisure to enjoy the world about them. They develop patience and calmness. Their conservatism is restful. Their nerves are not ajangle.

They are proud. May they hold tight the things of which they may be justly proud.

They do not want to leave their mountains. Their whole experience and interest is there. They love the land. They enjoy the care of their stock. They glory in the turn of the seasons, the coming of the springtime with its annual rebirth of hope and the fragrance of freshly plowed fields; the harvesttime when all uncertainty is ended and they know; the winter when there is an abatement of labors, and there is nut gathering and sorghum boiling and the aroma of smoking meat. They have no desire to leave the land, poorly as it has treated them. It is the only life they know—and maybe next year they will fare better.